BOYS HOME
LAKE WACCAMAW, N.C.
VISITORS WELCOME

Marina,

Thank you for bringing your excellent training skills to the staff and children of Boys and Girls Homes of NC. Because of you, children and staff will have brighter futures. As our founder, A. D. Peacock, recognized the need for a "sanctuary" for children in 1954 in eastern North Carolina he told himself, "If no one else will tackle the job, you must do it. Exactly how, I don't know. But with God's help, you will find a way."

God has continued to help us "find a way" through bringing very special people like you into our lives... into the lives of the staff and children at Boys and Girls Homes.

Thank you friend for becoming a part of our organization and community. Thank you for all you have done to "make a difference in this one organization" which will, no doubt, make a positive impact on the lives of countless numbers of children. Because of you, this "safe haven" is now better prepared to be a true "sanctuary" for HOPE and ENCOURAGEMENT.

May God bless you as you have blessed us.

Gary Faircloth
President / CEO
March 21, 2013

While walking along the shores of the ocean of life, a man saw someone in the distance leaning down, picking something up, and gently holding it in his arms.

As he came closer, he saw thousands of children being tossed violently onto the shore by the tides of social ill and human misery. Unable to return to the ocean of life on their own, the children were dying, if not physically, then emotionally, their promise as a member of society snuffed out. He observed a young man, A. D. was his name, picking up the children one by one, comforting them, and holding them tenderly in his arms.

After watching the seemingly futile effort to rescue the children, the observer protested, "A. D., there must be thousands of children on this beach. It would be impossible for you to save all of them. What can you do?"

The young man smiled as he picked up another of the suffering children. "I'll build a home where the children can be protected, nurtured, taught, and loved," he said, "and when they're ready, they can be returned to the ocean of life."

Still protesting, the man said to A. D., "To even think of doing something like this, you would have to be a fool. And to even attempt this, you'd be a damn fool. There are simply too many. You can't possibly save enough to make a difference."

A. D. carefully brushed off one of the struggling children and gently returned him to the ocean. "It made a difference to that one," he replied.

Adapted from *The Star Thrower* by Loren Eiseley

HUNTER

It Made a Difference to That One

The Realization of a Dream to Save Needy Children Through Boys & Girls Homes of North Carolina

The Staff of Boys & Girls Homes of North Carolina, Inc.
Bill Thompson, President
Larry Hewett
Sharon Connor
Paul Laird

The Donning Company Publishers

Title page images:
Top left: *Huntersville Cottage, named for the former Huntersville property near Charlotte, North Carolina, is one of the original buildings on the Boys Home property. It was converted to a cottage for girls in 1988 when the Huntersville campus for girls was closed. The first of the cottages for girls at the Lake Waccamaw campus, it is today home for as many as eight girls. Though not directly linked to a particular civic group, the girls' cottages receive support from the Extension & Community Association, the General Federation of Women's Clubs-North Carolina, the Women's Civic League, and churches.*
Top right: *Wakefield Cottage, built through a gift from Olaf and Rosa Atkinson Wakefield, was opened in 1995. Home today for eight girls, it is the second of the three cottages erected for girls at Boys and Girls Homes.*
Bottom left: *Stango Cottage, built through a gift from Vincent Stango in memory of his wife Catherine Jordan Stango, her parents John J. and Nettie Parker Jordan, her sister Lucille Jordan Bell, and her brother Richard Thomas Jordan, was dedicated September 5, 1996. It is the last of the cottages erected for girls at Boys and Girls Homes. Today, it is home for eight girls.*
Bottom right: *The Solomon Center was dedicated March 13, 2002, and was so named because of a gift by the late Adolph O. Solomon. Originally opened as a center for the emergency placement of children in danger of imminent harm, the center could house twenty children—ten boys and ten girls. Noted as an "awake care" facility, it was staffed around the clock with individuals who could monitor the children and be available for the placement of new children in the middle of the night, on weekends or holidays, or at other unusual times. A child could remain in the care of the center's staff for up to ninety days while his/her needs were assessed. Later, as this kind of care was phased out, the center became a part of the regular residential placement facilities.*

Endsheet: *"In the years to come...I can look up into the face of my Master and say, 'I did my level best that boys like this would have someone who wanted them.'" Quote attributed to A.D. Peacock when reading about a young man in trouble with the law.*

The Donning Company Publishers
184 Business Park Drive, Suite 206
Virginia Beach, VA 23462

Steve Mull, *General Manager*
Barbara Buchanan, *Office Manager*
Pamela Koch, *Editor*
Stephanie Danko, *Graphic Designer*
Amy Thomann, *Imaging Artist*
Mary Ellen Wheeler, *Proofreader*
Lori Kennedy, *Project Research Coordinator*
Scott Rule, *Director of Marketing*
Stephanie Linneman, *Marketing Coordinator*

B. L. Walton Jr., *Project Director*

Library of Congress Cataloging-in-Publication Data

It made a difference to that one : the realization of a dream to save needy children through Boys and Girls Homes of North Carolina / the staff of Boys and Girls Homes of North Carolina ; Bill Thompson, president ... [et al.].
p. cm.
ISBN-13 978-1-57864-332-5 (hardcover : alk. paper)
ISBN-10 1-57864-332-5 (hardcover : alk. paper)
1. Boys and Girls Homes of North Carolina. 2. Children--Institutional care--North Carolina--Lake Waccamaw. 3. Children with social disabilities--Services for--North Carolina--Lake Waccamaw. 4. Poor children--Services for--North Carolina--Lake Waccamaw. 5. Child welfare--North Carolina--Lake Waccamaw. I. Thompson, Bill, 1943 Sept. 18- II. Boys and Girls Homes of North Carolina.
HV743.L352B69 2006
362.73'2--dc22

2005028234

Printed in the United States of America at Walsworth Publishing Company

Contents

Foreword

On the Fiftieth Anniversary Observance of Boys and Girls Homes of North Carolina—Bill Thompson, President

I am sure all of you have read about the medieval knights and their quests. Knights like Miguel de Cervantes' Don Quixote de la Mancha—the Man of La Mancha who sought the impossible dream—and the Knights of the Round Table, who left King Arthur's court in search of the Holy Grail.

Somehow, I saw an analogy there among the quests and the dreams and Boys and Girls Homes. The quests and the dreams were a metaphor for our history.

I saw A. D. Peacock as Don Quixote, a man who dreamed of a place to care for orphaned boys. As with Don Quixote, people thought him crazy, that to reach such a goal was impossible and to attempt such a quest was foolish.

I saw Rube McCray like King Arthur, rallying the knights of the civic clubs to join him in his quest to build a home for unfortunate children. I saw other knights take up the quest: Slim Dallas and Dan Todd, Gilbert Marsh and Sloan Gibson, Judge Coleman Cates, and many others whose names are memorialized on plaques in the fellowship hall of the Boys and Girls Homes chapel like battered shields of great knights in the castle hall.

I heard their clarion call to thousands of people over the last fifty years to join in their quest to bind up the emotional and physical wounds of abused children, to shine the light of education on the darkness of ignorance, to lift up the fallen spirits of children who dared not even dream at all. And the response to the call to join the quest was so great that the quest became a crusade.

Theirs was, indeed, a noble quest, a search filled with hope and guided by determination and commitment. As I look at the challenges that face us now, I have to consider the challenges those early knights faced in building Boys and Girls Homes, and I realize that they faced those daunting challenges without the heritage that we now share.

Today we share their dream, not an impossible dream, but a possible dream. I believe that our goal is still worthwhile, and the need is still great. I believe that what has been accomplished is only a precursor of what is to come. I am personally honored to join in the quest.

Boys & Girls Homes *Logo*

Debbie Conway, who currently resides in Whiteville, North Carolina, and teaches art in the Whiteville school system, designed the Boys and Girls Homes of North Carolina logo. The original design contained only the children. Later, the wording "Boys and Girls Homes of North Carolina, Inc." was added for more specific identification of Boys and Girls Homes. When asked to recall designing the logo, Debbie said, *"I think I did that in about 1978 or '79! We* [she and husband Rob who was an employee of B&GH at the time] *came to Boys Homes in 1976, and I was pregnant with (our oldest child) Chris and stayed home with him and then Laura, too. I was glad to have something to do relating to art, and I did a few things for the development department. I have forgotten who asked me to do it, but they wanted something that was representative of all children. I think that they had just started taking girls at the Huntersville campus—thus the girl in the logo. At the time I did it, I didn't dream that they would still be using it almost twenty-five years later! I don't think I modeled the faces after any residents there then; I think I just made up generic faces. That's about all I can recall about it—I remember that I was surprised to see it used on so many things—I think they told me they wanted it for letterhead."*

The logo continues to represent Boys and Girls Homes on stationery, displays, vehicles, etc., and most prominently, a tiled version on the back wall of the stage in the William Horney Fellowship Hall of the Leamon Rogers Memorial Chapel. The logo is illuminated by spotlights during meetings and serves as a beautiful representation of the Homes. A special design used during the 2003–2004 years was created to celebrate the Homes' fifty years of service to children.

The story of Boys and Girls Homes is not about a place, an institution, or a program. More than that, it is about people and their dreams—dreams envisioned, dreams lost, and dreams restored. It is about the people who have dreams, those who dare to fulfill their dreams, those whose dreams are revived, and those who help to make dreams come true. It is about the children whose lives were touched by Boys and Girls Homes and whose dreams were restored as a result. It is about people and their willingness to build a home for children through their involvement and their resources and those who continue to support it. It is also about those who worked day to day with the children to support them and serve them, often acting as a mother, father, or grandparent, and always seeking to restore within the children dreams that had been

A. D. Peacock

There are many people who make up the Boys and Girls Homes' story. Literally thousands have pages, even chapters, in this story, and it is impossible to be fair to them all. With that said, however, our story begins with *the dreamer*, Mr. A. D. Peacock, who had established a funeral business in Whiteville, North Carolina, in the 1940s. His experiences as an undertaker caused his heart to ache for children left alone and without dreams because of the death of family members and the disruption of the family unit that often resulted. In addition to the emotional pain caused by the loss, the death of one of the parents was often financially devastating to the family or left the surviving parent so distraught that resorting to drugs or alcohol ensued and they became unable to parent. Sometimes, both parents would die, leaving the child without anyone. By his admission, Peacock was unable to erase the images of such children from his memory. Nor could he treat such children with indifference. He was deeply touched by their feelings of loss and despair, and he resolved to do something to help them and any others who might find themselves in need of guidance and direction.

In his book, *To Save a Boy*, Peacock describes an encounter that led him to begin turning his dream of helping children into a reality. *"On a late October afternoon in 1954 I took the body of a mother of four boys and three girls to the family home in the Western Prong community. The body was to remain in the front room of the home until the funeral services set for the following day. The weather was cold, with the hint of a hard frost or freeze in the air, and everything from the leafless trees to the early sunset suggested that winter would soon be here. It was more than the bleak weather and landscape, however, that sent a chill to my heart as I entered that house. I had seen much misfortune, and I knew that this family was indeed needy. In no way, though, was I prepared for what I now saw. In order to keep warm, the seven children had gone to bed, their only cover being ragged quilts and burlap bags ripped open and spread across the bed. They had gone to bed hungry, for there was no food in the house. In the small shabby living room, where I placed the mother in her casket, I noticed a small tin heater, but no wood to start a fire. Nor was there any to burn in the old-fashioned cook stove, had any food been available to the youngsters. The father? Perhaps he would show up later. Perhaps not. No one was at home except seven cold, hungry children—all between four and twelve years old—and their mother lying in a casket. As my eyes took in the loveless, desolate surroundings and the children's predicament, the old feeling of helplessness, now stronger than ever, settled over me like a pall. With an effort I shook it from me, and as I left that house, I knew I had to take some kind of action—and fast."*[1]

His commitment to action inspired the involvement of others, notably civic club members, which resulted in the eventual formation of Boys Home and later, Boys and Girls Homes of North Carolina. Peacock went on to describe what happened after leaving the children that evening.

"On my way back to Whiteville, I mentally formed a rough plan. I knew the Civitans were meeting that evening. I was already late, but hurriedly parked my car and ran into the meeting room. As I now recall the scene, I once again believe that what happened then must have been preordained, for on that very night the organization had chosen to discuss what it might do to make the children of some destitute family happy at Christmastime. The chairman had

The Kochtitzky Gymnasium and Boys and Girls Homes School on the Boys and Girls Homes campus was constructed ca. 1965 in memory of Edward Hugh Kochtitzky of Mt. Airy, North Carolina. Originally constructed as a gym/library, the gym continues to be one of the finest in the area. The library contained four classrooms that could be used for independent study and small group work. Later, the library was converted to an elementary school so that children in grades four through eight could attend school on campus. Consequently, the children more easily transitioned from their homes to residency at Boys and Girls Homes, and the smaller number of children enabled the Homes teaching staff to consider the individual needs of the children. The Boys and Girls Homes School is a unique entity in that it is a part of the Columbus County Public School System and is attended by residents of Boys and Girls Homes. A principal; English, mathematics, science, and social studies teachers; a physical education instructor; an auto mechanics instructor; and a woodworking instructor staff the school. Not only are the children able to develop their academic abilities, they have opportunities to explore areas of vocational interest such as woodworking, small engine repair, auto repair, electrical wiring, welding, and sheet metal working. Children can participate in organized physical activities such as basketball and volleyball in the gymnasium, which also serves as a venue for large group meetings, cultural events, and artistic performances.

barely announced the subject when I jumped to my feet. 'Gentlemen, I think I have the project...but we can't wait until Christmas.' I then told them about the seven children in Western Prong. As I described their desperate need, the Civitans forgot their unfinished meals—or maybe they had lost their appetites—to listen with something akin to spellbound horror. The exact, right words seemed to spring to my tongue as I continued. They accomplished what I had hoped for, affecting the members deeply. When I had finished, the Civitan president rose and told two of the members to stand by the door, and for the others as they left, to drop whatever they felt they could afford into a proffered hat. The proceeds would go to help the children. A count of the money, after the last member had contributed, totaled $176!"[2] Peacock's story that evening to the Civitan members and their eventual action to collect money to help those needy children if not realistically, then symbolically, led to the formation of Boys Home and the beginnings of a program of care that would bring the dream Peacock held to fruition.

1. *To Save a Boy, The Story of Boys Home, North Carolina,* by A. D. Peacock as told to Edward Uhlan. New York: Exposition Press, 1971.
2. Ibid.

Founding & Early Years

Turning the Dream into a Reality

Turning his dream of a haven for children into a reality would mean someone would have to lead the way. But who? In his own words, Peacock often conversed with himself about the need for such a place and who might take it on. He told of a time when he had a heart-to-heart talk with himself and said, "If no one else will tackle the job, you must do it. Exactly how, I don't know. But with God's help, you will find the way." It would also mean the involvement of others. So Peacock again went to the Whiteville Civitan Club and convinced the program chair to allow him to speak to the group. After an impassioned speech to implore the Civitan members to take on the establishment of a home for homeless youngsters, they agreed that it was a worthy project. Peacock told them it would have to occur one step at a time, and the first step would be to establish a home for boys and then develop one for girls. The vote on whether to consider such a project was affirmative. But not everyone was sold on it. One member commented: "Anyone who would think of doing something like this in a small town like Whiteville would be a fool, and anyone who attempted it would be a damn fool.

A. D. Peacock, center, with some members of the founding Board of Trustees for Boys Home. C. Bion Sears is standing behind Peacock's right shoulder. Other members include, left to right: Carl Ray, Sam Whitehead, Mrs. Hobson Sanderlin, Bill Floyd, Sears, W. Crowell Black, James L. Collier, and Martin Schulken.

Nevertheless, a feasibility committee was established and was asked to report back to the club at its next meeting. The committee's report was favorable, and on December 12, 1954, North Carolina Secretary of State Thad Eure chartered Boys Home of North Carolina. The members of this committee (Peacock, James L. Collier, Lee J. Greer, Martin Schulken, W. Crowell Black, Paul Williamson, W. F. Floyd, and Dr. Sam Whitehead) became charter members of Boys Home and helped guide Peacock through its establishment. A Board of Trustees for Boys Home was formed with Peacock, H. B. Floyd, R. G. Maultsby, W. F. Floyd, W. Crowell Black, Paul J. Williamson, P. F. Newton, James L. Collier, Martin Schulken, Lee J. Greer, C. Bion Sears, and Dr. Sam Whitehead, all of Whiteville and all members of the Civitan Club. An interesting if not amusing story about these first trustees concerns an encounter between Peacock and C. Bion Sears. It is said that Peacock went to Sears, president of First National Bank in Whiteville, many, many times to ask him to serve as one of the trustees for the Home. Sears would tell Peacock, "It isn't going to work!" But in addition to being a great dreamer, Peacock was persistent. Finally, on one of his visits, Sears inquired of Peacock, "A. D., just tell me, why do you want me to be on the board?" Peacock told him, "Well, I need someone to cover my checks!" Sears, moved by his honesty, agreed to serve and was indeed asked on occasion to "cover my checks!"

Finding the funds to operate the Home was an ongoing venture and one that was hinged on faith. Peacock would resort to all sorts of means to get operating money. In that day, tobacco was a major business in the area. Farmers gathered their crop and prepared it for market, a process that involved tying the cured leaves of tobacco into "hands" and putting them on a "grading stick." When taken to the market, these tied hands would be transferred to piles on baskets and placed in rows for the auctioneers and buyers to work with. Often, a hand of tobacco would fall off the pile. Peacock would go to the market, gather up the stray hands and leaves, make his own pile and sell it, and use the money to help with the operation of the Home.

The intensity of Peacock's dream to help children was matched only by his earnest research into the field of childcare. He traveled extensively, going to some thirty states and to many agencies that provided care for children, talking with those who were involved, to learn about operating a childcare facility. He consulted with, among others, J. Ardell Nation of Boys' Estate, Bill James of Boys Town in St. James, Missouri (Civitan Cottage at Boys and Girls Homes is an exact duplicate of a cottage at Boys Town), and Father Flanagan of the world-famous Boys Town of Omaha, Nebraska.

After considerable study, Peacock was ready to secure property on which to develop the Home. He thought he had a donor for some farm property located in Whiteville but was disappointed when that failed to materialize. Soon after, the members of his board found another piece of property near Whiteville and began working to clear it. But this too proved to be a disappointment, and soon they were looking for another site for the dream they shared with Peacock. Eventually, they came across an old home at Lake Waccamaw called the Gault House. It was situated right next to Lake Waccamaw and came with sixteen acres of land. Right away, Peacock and the other members of the board began to sense that they had found what they were looking for! Though Peacock didn't have the funds in hand with which to purchase this property, he felt the Lord would provide and set about getting things in place that would allow for children to be served there. It would prove to be a wonderful commitment!

Flemington Hall (the Gault House) was the first home for children at Boys and Girls Homes.

The house now serving as the administration building of Boys & Girls Homes of North Carolina and known as "Flemington Hall" was designed and built in 1924–25 by Mr. and Mrs. Francis Beers Gault. Mr. Gault was a native of St. Peter, Minnesota. He came to visit his granduncle, Charles Oscar Beers, in 1897 at Lake Waccamaw and remained after becoming involved in the family lumber business. Mr. Gault became president of the North Carolina Lumber Company and saw that the choicest lumber was set aside at his mill in Hallsboro for a number of years in anticipation of building the house. In the majority of its construction, he insisted upon double the support or size of timbers usually used including the doubling of the shingles with which the sides of the house are covered.

Mr. James B. Lynch of Wilmington, North Carolina, was the architect who drew the plans, but Mr. Gault served as his own contractor and actively supervised construction during the two years it took to complete the house. His brother, an electrician in Chicago, drew the electrical plan, and Mr. Sam T. Weaver of Lake Waccamaw installed most of the plumbing including the steam-heating system. Other local and nearby workmen performed most of the carpentry, brickwork, plastering, painting, etc. All of the floors were finished in their natural wood color, and all windows and doors were fitted with pure copper screens.

The pecan grove had been planted in 1913, and originally the hill overlooking the lake dropped off northward into the grove. The highway along the railroad (now NC Rte. 214) was being built, and Mr. Gault rented some of their earth-moving equipment and pushed part of the crest of the hill down into the swamp toward the lake to fill it in and the rest back around the new house to raise and level off the surrounding yard. Tennis courts were later added to this area.

In 1924, a power line was run from Wilmington to Whiteville through Lake Waccamaw, and electricity was available in the area for the first time. Flemington Hall was among the first homes in Lake Waccamaw to be built with electrical wiring. (As recalled by Mr. Charles Beers Gault)

Through several unfortunate circumstances, including the dissolution of the North Carolina Lumber Company, the house was abandoned in 1954. Mr. Peacock came down to Lake Waccamaw to look over the property and later purchased the house and about sixteen acres of land for the sum of about $45,000! The campus was literally a jungle. Trees had grown up, and vines covered everything. Early residents reported that they could cross the entire campus without ever touching the ground. The boys did most of the early clearing after school and on weekends.

Prior to the establishment of the program on the Lake Waccamaw site, Peacock, acting as director for the Homes, employed A. B. and Gladys Dawsey (who already were helping underprivileged children by taking needy boys into their home in Whiteville) to keep the children in their home while he and the trustees looked for a location to build a home. The Dawseys were the right people at the right time to care for the boys. According to P. E. Dawsey, son of A. B. and Gladys, their home was a "good place to help the boys find themselves...." P. E. recalled a story about one of the boys staying with his parents who ran away from their home. Mr. Dawsey began looking for the boy,

A. B. and Gladys Dawsey, first caretakers for the boys of Boys Home.

The five boys in this photo were the first residents of Boys Home. They lived in the Gault House under the care of A. B. and Gladys Dawsey.

soon found him, and brought him back home. The boy was counseled and made to realize that if he didn't stay with the Dawseys, he was subject to being sent to a reformatory, not a good place! Later that night, as A. B. stood outside the boy's room, he overheard him praying, *"Lord, I know I've done wrong, but I have a feeling that when Mr. Dawsey was my age he may have done worse than me!"* (As told by P. E. Dawsey). By 1956, the trustees had located the house and property at Lake Waccamaw. A. B. and Gladys Dawsey moved their "family" to the "Gault House" (now Flemington Hall), becoming caretakers of the children in the "first" home for boys admitted to the campus at Lake Waccamaw. Mr. and Mrs. Dawsey and their children, along with the Boys Home boys, lived together in the Gault House. They had a wonderful time there with the boys, caring for them and teaching them character. The message Mr. and Mrs. Dawsey preached to the boys was, "You can make it!" One day, Mr. Dawsey went over to the farm to get some things to eat. Upon his return, the "family" heard the horn blowing on the truck. Thinking that he was calling them to come help with the foodstuffs, they went outside to find him slumped over the steering wheel of his truck. He had had a heart attack! Not long after, Mr. Dawsey's doctors convinced him that the stress of caring for the children was not good for his health, so he and his family left Boys Home to open a nursing home.

The Dream Becomes Real

Civic Clubs

From its earliest beginnings, the Homes had a good relationship with civic clubs and their members. As has already been noted, members of the Whiteville Civitan were greatly involved in the charter and formation of the Home. In this section, we observe the role civic clubs have played in the development of the Homes. We also examine the move to a more professional management of the Homes.

From 1954 to 1958, the Home was primarily under the direction of A. D. Peacock. However, much of his time was spent promoting the program and securing the funds for its operation. At times, there were doubts that the program could continue. At a March 1957 meeting of the trustees, one at which Peacock was not included, the members examined the financial reports and seemingly decided to abandon the dream! Stunned by their actions, Peacock, "flat broke," decided that he would drive to Boys Estate in Brunswick, Georgia, to seek a job. He was given one in public relations and finance, but on his return trip to Whiteville, his elation at becoming employed disappeared as he thought about what would happen to the boys at Lake Waccamaw. Stopping for coffee, he gained a fresh resolve to make his dream work and called the trustees together for another meeting, during which he laid out plans for strengthening the program, including his plan to expand the role of civic clubs in the dream.

Civitan

"My ears hear the cry of children and the call throughout the world for peace, guidance, progress, and unity."

A. D. Peacock and some of the first boys who lived at Boys Home, working on the foundation for the Civitan Cottage.

In 1955, A. D. Peacock addressed a meeting of the North Carolina Civitan in Winston-Salem. The Civitan was asked to make the support of Boys Home a statewide project. Even though a number of Civitan members spoke enthusiastically about the program, a lot of the members remained hesitant about such an ambitious project. The project was tabled until the annual meeting that was to be held in Goldsboro the following spring. Peacock attended that meeting along with Civitan Robert G. Maultsby, who was given a few minutes on the agenda to speak to the group. Maultsby, with an eloquence that touched the hearts of those in attendance, encouraged the members to live up to the Civitan motto: "Builders of Good Citizenship." His plea was favorably received, and the convention voted to adopt Boys Home as a statewide project. A committee was formed to plan and raise the funds to build a house at Boys Home that would be named Civitan Cottage.

The Civitan Cottage, ca. 1960, the first cottage built for children on the Lake Waccamaw campus. The long windows that were the standard of the architectural design of this building and later of the other boys' cottages were renovated so that their lower end was higher from the ground.

Peacock noted that many had worked diligently to raise the funds for the cottage and singled out Wesley Williams of Raleigh and secretary of the Raleigh Merchants Bureau as being particularly involved. Williams served as chairman of the fundraising committee. On a Saturday in October of 1956, the Civitan held a quarterly meeting in Whiteville and traveled to Lake Waccamaw following the meeting for the groundbreaking ceremonies for Civitan Cottage. It was quite an affair with several distinguished guests, including North Carolina Governor Luther Hodges, U.S. Senator Alton A. Lennon, attorney John J. Burney, Civitan Governor Taft White, and *State Magazine* editor Carl Goerch. In early 1958, Civitan Cottage was completed and was ready to begin serving as a home for up to sixteen boys at Lake Waccamaw. As can be seen, Civitan members have been intimately involved in the development of Boys and Girls Homes, moving it from dream to reality. Civitan members and clubs continue to support the children with their financial gifts and other donations, personal visits, presents at Christmas and birthdays, aid to attend college, and by the encouragement of others to lend their assistance.

Another significant event occurred in 1958. It was in that year that the trustees realized that they needed someone who could serve full-time as director to attend to the management and fund-raising duties required by the Home. Peacock, who served as director from 1954 to 1958, needed relief from the increasing demands of that position and to attend to his funeral business. Trustee R. G. Maultsby noted that a friend of his might be interested in working in the position, and the board asked Maultsby to bring him in for an interview. R. N. "Rube" McCray, who for several years had served as athletic director and football coach at the College of William and Mary and who was noted for his work with young people, was interviewed and then hired as director. Rube and his wife Hester moved to the campus in 1958 and together began working to bring the dream to reality. One of the things mentioned by Peacock in his book about that dark period in 1957 in which the dream of a home for children seemingly was but a vapor was that there needed to be more involvement by more civic clubs. McCray set about to make that a reality.

Lions

"We Serve"

Many North Carolina Lions and their wives were instrumental in making the dream of Boys and Girls Homes a reality. Daniel Todd of Whiteville, Bob Lee, Judge Coleman Cates, and Stacy Budd are some of those and are pictured in this photo. These men also served on the Board of Trustees for Boys Home. The Coleman Cates Award, named for Judge Cates, is presented to the Lions governors and Boys and Girls Homes district chairmen whose districts achieve specific goals.

In 1959, at their convention in Asheville, the Lions of North Carolina Multiple District 31 adopted Boys Home of North Carolina as a statewide project and began raising funds for the Lions Cottage on the Lake Waccamaw campus. That cottage for sixteen boys was completed in 1960, and a cottage at the Huntersville campus was built in 1972. Through the years, the Lions of North Carolina have been the largest civic organization in the state and, consequently, have contributed the largest total amount of money in support of Boys and Girls Homes. Lions have created more individual endowments than any other group. They use the endowments to honor extraordinary achievements by their membership.

Lions Cottage at Boys Homes provided a second home for sixteen boys on the Boys Home campus. The cottage was provided as a gift from the Lions of Multiple District 31 of North Carolina. Pictured are fifteen of the boys living in the cottage in 1960. Today the cottage is an integral part of the program of care for the children of Homes. It functions as a home for nine boys and serves as a cooking cottage for three other cottages on the campus.

As the number of boys increased at Boys Home, providing transportation for them became a pressing need. During the early years of the Home, transportation was primarily by car, station wagons to be exact. Later, buses became an integral part of the boys' transportation, and Lions clubs were generous in providing them for the Home. The Pinehurst Lions Club donated one of the earliest buses. In the photo above, the High Point Lions proudly display the bus they purchased for the Home.

Jaycees

"We believe...that service to humanity is the best work of life."

In this photo, Jaycees of North Carolina make a visit to Boys and Girls Homes. The young men at the front are President Jim Hastings and Chairman of the Board of Jaycees Bill Hobbs. Jaycees have traditionally visited the campus to visit with the children and hold district meetings.

In 1961, the North Carolina Junior Chamber of Commerce (Jaycees) undertook a campaign to raise funds for a Jaycee cottage on the Lake Waccamaw campus. One of the major efforts in that regard was the establishment and operation of the North-South All-Star Football Game played annually at Ficklen Stadium at East Carolina University. The host chapter, the Greenville Jaycees, invited the top high school senior football players from across North Carolina to participate in the game. The game not only helped raise funds for Boys and Girls Homes but brought immeasurable public recognition as well. As a result of the game and other projects, Jaycee Cottage was completed in 1962. Although the game was discontinued in 1979, Jaycees continue to support Jaycee Cottage and its residents with financial assistance, visits to the campus (including holding their spring Executive Committee meeting at Boys and Girls Homes), inviting residents to chapter meetings and activities, observing birthday celebrations, and purchasing Christmas gifts.

The North Carolina Jaycees constructed Jaycee Cottage in 1962 as a gift to the Homes.

This photo of the Boys and Girls Homes amphitheater with Lake Waccamaw in the background shows members of the community, visitors to Lake Waccamaw, and Boys and Girls Homes residents enjoying a music performer at one of the Homes' many presentations of artists from across North Carolina and other areas. The stage is still functional and can be quickly readied for use. For years, Boys and Girls Homes has provided its residents with opportunities to experience first hand the talents of amateur and professional entertainers while inviting members of the community and visitors to Lake Waccamaw to share the events. In the mid-seventies, United Carolina Bank (which later merged with BB&T) provided funds through its trust department to bring entertainers to the campus. As the years progressed, a variety of agencies, foundations, and trusts have funded various performers to visit the campus and share their talents with the children and community.

Kiwanis

"Serving the Children of the World"

Kiwanis Cottage 2004. The cottage was opened in 1964 and served as a home for sixteen boys. In this photo, the cottage is sporting a new roof funded and installed by the members and clubs of the Carolinas District.

The Carolinas District of Kiwanis International became involved in the support of Boys Home in the fall of 1961 when two members of the High Point Kiwanis Club, Gilbert Marsh and Sloan Gibson, met with Boys Home administration to discuss the possibility of building a Kiwanis cottage on the Lake Waccamaw campus. Subsequent to that meeting, those two men enlisted the help of J. Sanders Dallas Sr., also of High Point, to raise the funds for the construction of the Kiwanis Cottage. By soliciting the involvement of fellow Kiwanian William Horney and other Kiwanis clubs throughout the district, the cottage was completed in 1964. Their junior members, Circle K, Key Club, and Builders Club, have joined Kiwanians in their efforts to support the Homes. Members of the Key Club have made the Homes their district project and have been instrumental in recent years in meeting the transportation needs of the campus, purchasing both a van and a bus.

In this picture taken in 1963, members of the Carolinas District of Kiwanis pose at the site of the future Kiwanis Cottage on the campus of Boys Home.

2005–2006 Key Club Governor Greg Jones, member Jamie Rau, and Secretary Christina Harris proudly display a twenty-five-passenger bus provided by the Carolinas District Key Club, a sponsored youth organization of Kiwanis International. Carolinas District Key Club members, high school students from across North and South Carolina, secured the funds for the vehicle through their "Keys to the Vans" program, a project to provide transportation for the children of the Homes.

Rotary

"Service—in the community, in the workplace, and throughout the world."

Rotary Cottage was constructed as a gift from the Rotary districts of North Carolina in 1966.

W. D. Welch (left) presents Rube McCray with the first Rotary Cottage building fund check, ca. 1962.

In the mid-1960s, several Rotary club districts in North Carolina, at the urging of Ben Southerland of Wilmington, took on the challenge of building a cottage on the Boys Home campus. It was completed and dedicated in 1966. Many districts continue to support the maintenance of the cottage and the welfare of the boys who live there. Rotary members instituted "Rotary Harvest Day" as a time to visit Boys and Girls Homes and bring items for the cottage.

Optimist

"Bringing Out the Best in Kids"

The Optimist Cottage at Lake Waccamaw, established in 1968, was constructed as a home for twenty boys with contributions from Optimists of North Carolina.

Many of the funds for Optimist Cottage were raised during a telethon conducted by WWAY-TV3 in Wilmington. Several television celebrities participated in the telethon. Pictured here, Ed Nelson, who played Dr. Michael Rossi on the television series Peyton Place, *joins in a meal for the participants of the telethon.*

In 1967, the North Carolina Optimist District undertook the project of building a cottage for twenty boys on the Lake Waccamaw campus. A telethon was held on WWAY-TV in Wilmington that raised over $60,000 to begin construction. The Optimists also built a cottage for the program at Huntersville in 1974. Optimists continue to be active in contributing to the operation and maintenance of the Lake Waccamaw cottage. In 2003, Optimists in North Carolina achieved their $1 million endowment goal, the first of the civic groups to reach this goal.

Optimists at the dedication ceremony for Optimist Cottage at Lake Waccamaw, ca. 1968. Left to right: Grover Richey, Bobby Howell, Dr. Carl Bowen, Chip Keziah, unidentified, H. B. Stroup, unidentified.

The Lang Vocational Building on the Boys and Girls Homes Campus has long been a center of activity for the children of the Homes. It is a multiuse facility that has provided numerous services to the Homes during its history. The building has one large room (far right) that has been used as a center for campus mailings and recordkeeping and, in recent years, as a conference center and a theater for movies and other entertainment events. The building also contains a shop area (center) that is used as a teaching/working station for woodworking, small engine repair, auto mechanics, metalworking, welding, and electrical wiring. Another room in the building (left rear) is used for the storage and distribution of foodstuffs, including coolers and freezers for meats and other chilled foods, school supplies, and toiletries. The upper floor of the building contains the offices and meeting facilities for the Boys and Girls Homes Family Foster Care/Adoption Services.

General Federation of Women's Clubs of North Carolina

"Dedicated to community improvement by enhancing the lives of others through volunteer service."

General Federation of Women's Clubs members participate in the support of the programs for the children at Boys and Girls Homes. Here, members of the Fuquay-Varina GFWC-NC have set up refreshments in the Girls Activity Center in observance of St. Patrick's Day. In addition to their financial support, GFWC-NC members visit and mentor the children, an important way of enhancing their lives.

The General Federation of Women's Clubs is a faithful supporter of Boys and Girls Homes' efforts to help children. Not only do they give financially to support the programs of care for the children, they visit the campus, interacting especially with the young women to celebrate birthdays and conduct leadership workshops. Additionally, GFWCNC junior and senior members bring toiletries, computer equipment, and computer supplies for the girls at the Homes during their visits. Members of the group are involved in a "Keep the Flame of Hope Burning" campaign to raise funds to help cover the operating costs of the Homes.

North Carolina Extension & Community Association

"Strengthening Families"

ECA members and Boys and Girls Homes Board of Trustees member Carolyn Register, right with folder in arm, bring fellow ECA associates and other community individuals for a visit to the Homes. Sharing with others the work of the Homes is another of the many ways civic club members offer support.

The North Carolina Extension and Community Association has played a special role in the development of Boys and Girls Homes. Its predecessor organization, the North Carolina Extension Homemakers Association, was one of the early supporters of Girls Haven of North Carolina when it was located in Asheboro. Following the merger of Boys Homes of North Carolina and Girls Haven of North Carolina, ECA and its members led the effort to expand the girls' campus at Lake Waccamaw. Today, ECA members visit the campus to spend time with the children and provide items such as toiletries, school supplies, food, and equipment for the cottage and activity center.

Other Civic Club Involvement

There are other civic groups that have been a part of developing and supporting the dream of Boys and Girls Homes. They include the Ruritan and the Women's Auxiliary of Veterans of Foreign Wars. These groups provide financial assistance and in-kind gifts that support the Homes' efforts to make a difference in the lives of the children.

Girls Haven & the Move to Huntersville

This old newspaper clipping is of the Meacham property on the Huntersville Campus, which was initially established as a residence for ten boys and their teaching parents. Another clipping noted that the Optimist Cottage would soon be licensed to house twelve girls.

Initially, Boys Home of North Carolina was that—a home for boys. An early promotional piece, however, depicts a little girl saying to A. D. Peacock, "What about me?" as her twelve-year-old brother was being taken from their home for a trip to Boys Home at Lake Waccamaw. Peacock is to have said, "Since that day, I've worried a lot about whatever happened to her." For years, he tried to interest individuals or organizations in providing facilities and programs where both boys and girls could be served. In November 1970, Peacock, his brother Randall, and a small group of citizens met and agreed to form such an organization. From that meeting, a program called Girls Haven was begun in Burnsville, North Carolina. The program received its charter on December 8, 1970, with Randall Peacock serving as its first director. Girls Haven was conceived to provide the kind of family

The Civitan Cottage at Huntersville.

atmosphere needed to help disadvantaged girls become responsible, productive members of society. The goal was to have a Girls Haven program in each congressional district in the state. On May 5, 1973, a planned Girls Haven facility in Asheboro held its groundbreaking. The program for the event listed special guests A. D. Peacock of Boys Home, Mrs. Lark Newsom of the Federation of Women's Clubs (GFWC-NC), Adam Thompson, state director of VICA, and David Flaherty. The Executive Committee for the Girls Haven program included Amos Butler (chairman), David Parker (president), John Kaplafka (vice president), Mrs. Lark Newsom (public relations), Ogburn Yates, Bill Martin (executive director), and Mrs. Louis Johnston (executive secretary). The Girls Haven program officially moved to Asheboro in 1974, and the first girls were admitted to the campus that had been established there on July 17, 1976.

In March 1970, Boys Home of North Carolina had acquired 124.22 acres of land and the Meacham cottage located on it in the Huntersville community north of Charlotte for $124,200 and had expanded its program for boys to include that campus. Houseparents Mr. and Mrs. W. T. (Tupper) Wingfield and the first ten boys moved to the Huntersville campus in August 1970.

According to reports, the Girls Haven program struggled to exist. When an offer was made to consolidate with Boys Homes of North Carolina, it was accepted, and Boys and Girls Homes of North Carolina, Inc., was born. In August 1980, after the merger with Girls Haven, the boys living on the Huntersville campus were moved to the Lake Waccamaw campus, and the Girls Haven operation was relocated from Asheboro to the Huntersville facility.

Prior to the merger with Girls Haven, facilities to accommodate services at Huntersville had been added. In 1972, the North Carolina Lions constructed Lions Cottage, the North Carolina Civitan constructed Civitan Cottage in 1974, and the North Carolina Optimists constructed Optimist Cottage in 1979. To provide the children with opportunities for athletics and recreation, a recreational facility named for the late R. N. McCray was constructed in 1979.

The R. N. McCray Athletic Facility at Huntersville was considered a "first class" facility for athletics.

In August 1988, needing to streamline operating costs, the two programs of childcare were consolidated into one operation on the campus at Lake Waccamaw. The Huntersville campus was closed and in February 1990 was sold. To accommodate the girls' program, major renovations were made to a historic farmhouse (now Huntersville Cottage) on the Lake Waccamaw campus, and Girls Haven became a part of the program at Lake Waccamaw. Today, it includes Huntersville Cottage, Wakefield Cottage, Stango Cottage, and the Bill-Will Cooper Girls Activity Center.

Life at the Homes

Not only did the children participate in athletics at school, they enjoyed participating on campus teams in intramural activities. In this photo, the boys have an afternoon basketball practice session.

Living the dream at Boys and Girls Homes was much like living in the "average" American home, as much as it could be. It was intended to be that way! The feeling was that the children who came to the Homes should be given every opportunity to live as normal a lifestyle as could be provided. That was the reason the cottages were designed and managed much like a typical home, containing a living area, dining area, kitchen, laundry, recreation room, and bedrooms. The founders did not want the cottages to be dorm-like or set up like penal facilities. And the adults living with the children were called "house parents" or in today's vernacular, "teaching parents"—with the emphasis on "parents." The routines were similar to those of a typical home, with the children having set times for family-style meals, study, recreation, sleeping, waking, and most of all, chores. As has been previously noted, the first parents were Mr. and Mrs. A. B. Dawsey, who were already keeping children in their home in Whiteville along with their own children.

No matter what, there always seemed time to gather for a group photo, as in this picture taken in 1959.

Dawseys were employed by A. D. Peacock to keep boys for Boys Home in Whiteville. When the Gault property at Lake Waccamaw was purchased, the Dawseys moved their family and the first five Boys Home boys to the lake. As the cottages were constructed, several of the first "parents" in those homes were retired grandmotherly ladies who were responsible for up to sixteen young men. Along with the counselors, they were many things to the boys including mother, father, grandparent, friend, etc. When one listens to the alumni of the Homes talk about their house parents, you can sense both a fondness and appreciation for the firmness the "parents" demonstrated as they watched over them. One former resident wrote, *"My brother...and I were residents at the Home back in 1966, and we were there for about five years. At the time we thought it was kind*

A group photo taken of the children, including some of the first girls to be a part of the program. Pictures in that day always required getting dressed up.

Athletics, whether school-related or campus-related, were a vital part of the children's development. Boys and Girls Homes has produced a number of terrific athletes. Boys Home boys enjoyed participating in athletics and played all sports at Hallsboro High School. Several members of the Hallsboro Tigers basketball team were Boys Home boys. One of the more outstanding Hallsboro athletes was Boys Home resident, football player Randy Ward. In one night, Randy scored four touchdowns, although one was called back because of a penalty. Boys and Girls Homes residents continue to be involved in the athletic programs at their current high school, East Columbus.

of rough, but as we have had the time and years to reflect back on our time there, we both agree that had it not been for the Home we would have never made it in life. I have some really fond memories of the Boys Home, and I will never forget the wonderful people I was so fortunate to become acquainted with while there. The people of North Carolina are so very lucky to have such a place as the Boys and Girls Homes that their children can go to because it really turns out some of the finest citizens this country will ever know. I AM THANKFUL FOR THE MEMORIES!"

Many alumni express similar sentiments. Often they return to the Homes with their families to share the part of their lives that was Boys and Girls Homes. One former resident wrote this about his experiences: *"I was in the Jaycee Cottage during the...school year. At the time, I did not want to be there, as I was placed there against my will. As I grew older, I realized that being there at the Boys Home (as it was called then) was the best place in the world for me to be. I would imagine the House Parents at that time...have long retired. I learned a lot from those two people, and admire them for the contribution, as well as the sacrifices they made on the kids' behalf. I'd love to visit there and show my kids the things I remember from the area. From the pecan trees, to the horse*

Washday! With children, there are always clothes to wash. In the early days, there was a laundry on campus with large washers and dryers. Today, each cottage has its own equipment.

Horseback riding was another adventure many children experienced for the first time at the Homes. Several have become quite proficient, and for many, it is an excellent therapeutic tool.

ranch, to the big lake, it is truly a nice place, from what I remember."

The children endeared themselves to the house parents as well. Some time ago, a former parent wrote: *"Lately, I have found myself wondering about the boys that my husband and I cared for as house parents in the JC Cottage. So I looked to see if Boys and Girls Home of NC had a website and was delighted to find it. I see that my boy...was there for nine years. He was such a sweet child. I was not surprised at...success. He used to come in my back door at the JC Cottage (from the Lions Cottage). I would hear his astounding voice, clear back into the laundry room, break into a divine spiritual song. Bless his heart! Yes, I have many beautiful memories with my boys. I had to make sure that every one of them had a homemade birthday cake and small present. They would be overjoyed! Most of them had never even had a birthday cake, much less a present at that time. We also had a great time making Halloween costumes for the boys. We would go over to the Country Store, pick up bits and pieces and throw them together at the sewing machine, and most times, my boys would win the costume contest. I remember little..., we found him a tux with tails and made him a top hat, decorated with silver glitter.... He took first place for his age group. Then there was...we made into Frankenstein. Everyone loved it, even Mr. Ramey, the assistant director at the time. I still love looking at my old pictures of them. I just wonder if they ever think of us."*

In the early years of the Homes, calisthenics was a big part of campus life, for residents and staff!

Many children enjoyed music and demonstrated musical abilities as this photo illustrates. Capitalizing on the children's love for music later led to the formation of the famous Boys Home choirs.

Of course, the stories of life at the Homes, as the children worked, played, were disciplined, and even plotted to do the things young people do, seem at times larger than life. This is normal for all of us!

The pictures that follow offer some indication of the way life was/is at Boys and Girls Homes. Of course, it isn't possible to depict all activities, but, well, you get the point!

Life isn't all fun and games. Chores are a big part of life at the Homes. Here, Mrs. Maultsby gives this young man a lesson in cooking, something that was very important—if you and your cottage mates wanted to eat! Additionally, hungry children meant lots of cleanup from meals. The children were and are required to clean the kitchen, bathrooms, bedrooms, living room, and other areas of their home.

Athletics continue as a big part of campus life. Coach Rocco Wadsworth talks with this group about soccer.

In this photo, the boys are learning to use the arc welder to weld pieces of metal together to create a metal working project. The Lang Vocational Building provides an important place for the children to develop vocational interests.

Well, the carburetor could be messed up! These boys learn a little about tuning an engine as they work on this vehicle.

Recognizing the achievements of the children has always been important. It is a way of saying we care! And it gives the children a sense of confidence to learn that they can accomplish and excel. Here, Mr. McCray presents a trophy to Gene Cheek.

Keeping healthy sometimes meant a trip to the doctor, or campus nurse in this case. For a number of years, the Homes employed a nurse to attend to the children's injuries and illnesses. The local health clinic, doctors, and emergency rooms meet those needs today.

Athletic prowess and its recognition have provided many young people with a sense of belonging and have helped them become better citizens. Alan Canady (left) and Kyle Ramey (right) present awards to a young man who demonstrated outstanding athletic ability.

Developing talent in all areas has been an important part of life at the Homes. In this photo, Henry Sadler practices for his performance while another young man sets up for the annual talent show.

Education

by Bill Thompson

Study hall was part of the daily regimen on the campus. Often, the older children would tutor the younger ones.

From the very beginning of Boys and Girls Homes, education of the children has been one of the major elements of our program of care. As we look ahead, we commit ourselves to not only a renewed emphasis on the importance of education, but to an expansion of our effort to provide this essential element in the development of the children who come to us for care.

This commitment is based on our philosophy of care, which affirms that the direction in which education starts a child will determine his future. Many of the Boys and Girls Homes children were behind in their formal education when they arrived. It was like starting life with two strikes against them. It is the responsibility of the Homes to give them every tool they will need to overcome the obstacles that have been placed and will be placed in their path so that they may lead a more complete and useful life. A good, solid education is certainly one of these tools.

From its very beginning, the Homes staff have encouraged the children to develop their educational interests, and the pursuit of educational growth has been an important part of the campus life. Providing the children with an education may be the way out of the conditions that brought them to the Homes in the first place. This early photo shows boys getting off the bus. It is believed that the man at the front of the bus is Mr. McCray, who frequently met the boys after school to check on their progress. Today, the children in grades four through eight attend the Boys and Girls Homes School, a unique, on-campus elementary school funded by the Public Schools of North Carolina, the Columbus County Schools, and Boys and Girls Homes. Children of high school age attend the local public high school, an alternative school, or the community college in pursuit of their GED.

Former resident Robert Hardy, now a captain and test pilot on an EMJ-145 aircraft for American Eagle Airlines, wrote about the importance of education for him: "How has education played a role in my success? Well, there is absolutely no way I could have arrived at my current position in life without my education. Education gave me the tools needed to teach me how to fly airplanes and how to complete projects. It showed me how to set goals and complete those goals within deadlines."

We believe that education for our children is not just the accumulation of facts or the acquisition of data. Education is the never-ending assimilation of everything around them, the ability to sift through all that touches their lives so they can determine for themselves what is true and useful. A good education will allow our children to distance themselves from those elements of society that make decisions for them. A well-educated person cannot be dictated to in his decision-making process. Neither the drug pusher, the street thug, nor the pimp can make decisions for a truly educated person.

Real freedom and success can only come through academic and spiritual education. We hope in the process that our children also learn that education is not terminal. It is endless. It doesn't stop when they leave Boys and Girls Homes. If our past is an indicator of our future, then education at Boys and Girls Homes will continue to play a major role in the development of our children.

Life on the Farm

Chores on the farm allowed the children to expend some pent-up energy and emotions. It also permitted them to develop a sense of love and caring as they became attached to some of the animals. Having the hogs and cows on the farm was important also because they were a source of meat for hungry children. For a number of years, the meat was processed on the campus. The Homes continue to keep cattle that are used for beef purposes, but the meat is processed commercially today. Additionally, a garden of some size has always been a part of the farm, and gathering the fruits of the garden was important because they put food on the table in the cottages. For many years, a lot of the fruits and vegetables came mainly from the farm. A small garden is still a part of the farm but is more of a teaching tool than a source of vegetables.

One of the very unique aspects of Boys and Girls Homes is its campus. It is more than just a place to house children in institutional buildings devoid of character. Boys and Girls Homes has, in a way, always belonged to the children, in large part because they were involved in its construction and maintenance. Almost any gathering of alumni, especially of the earliest members, will certainly evoke some kind of discussion regarding their involvement in certain building or clearing projects. At one particular meeting, some of the former boys began to reminisce about their time at the Home. The discussion turned to "Rube," and it was remembered with affection how he would say "Boys, we're going to...today!" They remembered that it was "they" who did the work, but others with keener memory recalled that Mr. McCray always helped!

The farm is dotted with many pecan trees. Numerous trees were lost to storms during the summer of Hurricane Fran, but the Homes still boasts one of the largest pecan groves in North Carolina. Collecting the pecan nuts, a precious commodity, remains an important part of campus life. Selling the excess after keeping some to use in cooking and eating nets an important financial resource for the Homes.

The Boys and Girls Homes farm comprises a significant part of the campus and more than tripled the size of the campus when it was purchased. It has been a special part of the Homes, at one time providing many of the foodstuffs such as vegetables and meats used on campus. It was also a place to go to get away from "things" that one wanted to clear from one's past. And the recreational experiences were awesome. Tending to the pigs, cows, and horses were more than chores. It allowed many to learn to care for and love something that previously had not been a part of their way of life. Because it was so special to so many, it is important to include it in this story of the Homes.

The farm was bought in 1966 from the Sutton family. Mr. Sutton was a gentleman farmer. He had retired and much of the farm had not been kept up. Mr. McCray and Bill Thompson inquired about purchasing the farm from Mr. Sutton, who agreed that he would sell a parcel of about 100 acres for $1,000 dollars per acre. There were actually 108 acres, but Mr. Sutton consented to leave the agreement as it was stated. Mr. McCray originally thought that a hundred people could be found to donate $1,000 each to pay for the farm, but in 1966 that wasn't easy. They did find getting a thousand people to give $100 a lot easier, and that was how the farm was purchased.

These pictures offer a glimpse of the way life was and is on the farm. To a child, there is something very important about growing up on a farm. It can't be explained, it just is, and most of the better pictures remain in the minds of those who grew up on the farm!

Ronnie Burney smiles after corralling a calf. Calves have always been a part of the farm, and many of the young people have participated in 4-H stock contests as a result of their experiences.

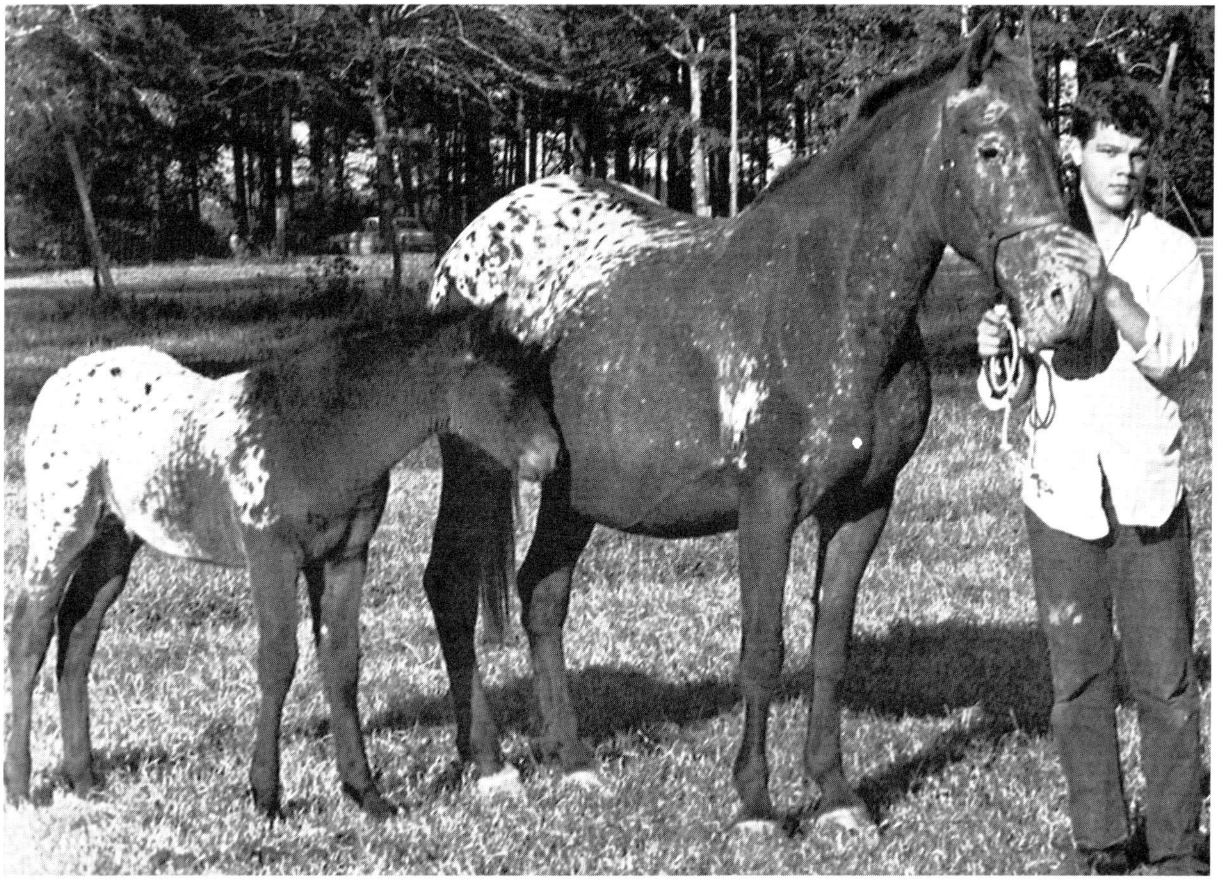

Volumes can be written about the positive effects of horses on children at the Homes. Many of the young people have never been around a horse. Tending to its care helps develop a sense of responsibility in the context of a caring relationship—an experience some of the children may never have had.

Former resident Elton Locklear prepares to show his horse at the 2004 Fall Festival at the Boys and Girls Homes Exhibition Center and arena. Horses have long played a role in the lives of the children of the Homes. The children learn to care for the animals and develop their horsemanship skills, often participating and scoring well in local and regional horse shows and riding events.

This aerial photo shows the Boys and Girls Homes Exhibition Center (and accompanying horse stalls), which is located at the heart of the farm, attracting many people to campus as it serves as a venue for as many as thirty shows each year.

In this photo, boys can be seen working on the site of the arena project that was sponsored by the Lake Waccamaw Lions.

One of the more outstanding features of the farm today is the Boys and Girls Homes Exhibition Center. This covered arena with its fifty thousand square feet of floor space is the venue for numerous activities including musical events (gospel, bluegrass, drama, contemporary gospel, etc.), car shows, dog shows, horse shows, rodeos, wild game cook-offs, and a variety of meetings. Initially developed by the Lake Waccamaw Lions, the Homes took it over in 1993, determined to improve and expand it as the catalyst for a major fundraising program. Many of the people who were to become supporters of the Homes learned about its work when they came to the Exhibition Center for an event. Income from the use of the facilities reverts to the operating budget for the programs of care. The Exhibition Center also provides the children with a place to work and experience recreational activities such as horseback riding.

The Country Store

Country Store Manager Doris Wagner hangs a sign indicating the new hours for the present-day Boys and Girls Homes Country Store. The store is open six days a week to receive and sell donated items.

A photo of the first Country Store ca. 1975, located just off old Highway 74-76 that ran in front of the Boys Homes campus.

Located near the farm is the Boys and Girls Homes Country Store. The Country Store is the Homes' outlet for excess donated goods and items that cannot be used directly by the children and so serves as a source of needed revenue. The items are placed in the store and sold to the general public. Many customers looking for an odd item or an exceptional bargain visit the store each year. Some customers make daily trips to the store to see what "new" items might have been added to the store's inventory. Donations to the store are tax deductible in accordance with IRS regulations.

The Chapel Ministry

by Bill Thompson

Attending church has always been a vital part of the program of care at the Homes. In this early photo, the boys are leaving services at one of the local churches.

From the very beginning of Boys and Girls Homes fifty years ago, spiritual development of the children has been a major part of the program of care. For many years, the children went to the various local churches and participated in their youth activities. On campus, the Homes held, and still holds, regular devotional services in each cottage. With the construction of the Leamon Rogers Memorial Chapel in 2001, the Homes now has a physical focal point for religious education and spiritual development. It is one of the best things done at the Homes and allows for expanding the emphasis on the development of the children's relationship to God.

Who am I? This young man may be pondering that question as he gazes at this figurine of an angel. Boys and Girls Homes has sought to help the children answer that and other questions as they seek to "develop a new story" through the chapel ministry.

But the chapel is not all that is needed to develop a child's relationship to God. That relationship has to be a part of every program on the campus. It has to be evident in the lives of each person who comes in contact with the children. All the rules and regulations, all the verbal and written instructions, cannot come as close to teaching children about God as does their observance of the behavior of the adults who are teaching them by example.

At Boys and Girls Homes, the children are exposed to well-trained, hardworking, dedicated, and caring people whose job is to help them recognize the problems that brought them here and to help them find ways to overcome those problems so that they can lead healthy, productive lives. But regardless of how smart the staff is or how much they care or how hard they work, there are times when they do not have the answer to the children's problems. That is why it is so important that every child who comes to the Homes, for even a short time, learns that there is an answer, that God does know their problems and that He, above all others, can give them the answer they need. It is the duty of the Homes to show them how to develop that relationship with God so that they can realize how He can help them.

As Vice President for Childcare Becky Wray noted, "We know that our belief about the importance of the children's relationship with God is more than just a feeling or belief that we hold." Becky writes: "Hardwired to Connect, a 2003 report to the nation from the Commission on Children at Risk, composed of thirty-three children's doctors, research scientists, and mental health and youth service professionals,

The Leamon Rogers Memorial Chapel at Boys and Girls Homes, dedicated September 30, 2001, provides a venue for the spiritual development of the children. The chapel contains both a sanctuary and fellowship hall. Both can accommodate 250 to 300 people for various activities. The entrance to the fellowship hall is at the rear, and the hall serves as a meeting place for a variety of functions. It has its own kitchen, bathrooms, emergency power, and water supplies and can serve as a shelter during inclement weather. One of the strong features of the spiritual ministry is its mentoring program. Children who desire are provided with adult mentors from the local community. These persons are trained to work with the children and serve as a friend and mentor to them. The chapel is not only a venue for the spiritual growth of the children, it provides a place for others to share their talents with them. Many artists have performed in the chapel for the children and the community, including noted blues and jazz performer Mojo Collins, through the Boys and Girls Homes Performing Arts Series.

recommends *'that youth-serving organizations purposely seek to promote the moral and spiritual development of children, recognizing that children's moral and spiritual needs are as genuine, and as integral to their personhood, as their physical and intellectual needs.'"* This is noteworthy for the following reason. For decades, youth services focused primarily on behavioral, emotional, intellectual, and psychological needs with minimal acknowledgment of their spiritual needs. This trend is now being reversed. Documented research in this report substantiates that children's neurological makeup predisposes them to seek spiritual connection to God. In essence, they are "hardwired to connect," and this drive for connection becomes a developmental need equally as important as physical and intellectual development.

Though the staff of Boys and Girls Homes did not necessarily have empirical scientific evidence to support a child's need for spiritual connection, they intuitively and experientially know that children must have their spiritual needs met if their lives are to be complete and purposeful. Therefore, church attendance has historically been a required part of the weekly schedule. With the recent addition of the chapel, more activities geared toward spiritual awakening and growth have been developed. These ministries provide wonderful opportunities for the children to become acquainted with God's loving plan for them. As research overwhelmingly shows that there is a clear correlation between youngsters' personal devotion to God and good outcomes, i.e., reduced risk-taking, greater regard for self and others, and a sense that life has meaning, the Homes is more motivated than ever to provide opportunities for its residents that will grow and challenge them spiritually.

Providing the children with the knowledge of God's unconditional love and teaching them how they can have access to God's wisdom is part of that mission.

Making the Dream Work

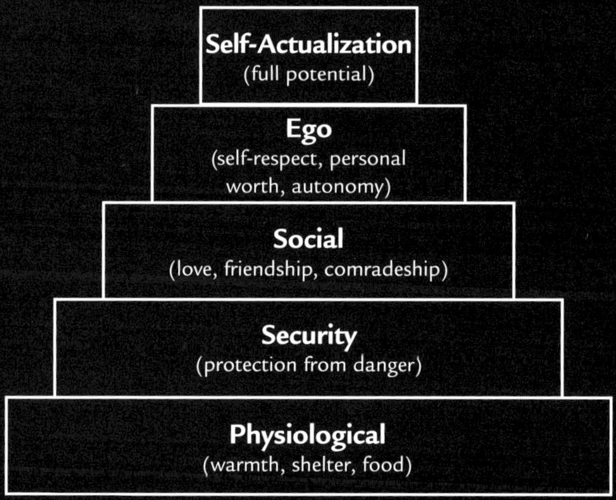

Maslow's Hierarchy of Needs

In this section, the programs and philosophy of meeting the needs of the children by the Homes are given a brief look. The first of these is the **Residential Program** (Cottage Care). For more than fifty years, Boys and Girls Homes' most prominent program has been its residential or cottage program. In its earliest years, there was an awareness of the problems facing children, and the staff tried in every way to help solve those problems. One of the most obvious solutions is to remove the child from an unhealthy situation and place him or her in a caring environment that provides for more normal growth. The child is then in a setting that seeks to meet what Maslow described as a "Hierarchy of Needs." Maslow's model is arranged in somewhat of a pyramid with the physiological need of warmth, shelter, and food forming the base and the need to achieve one's full potential at the top.

These young men appear to be engaged in evening study time in their bedroom, an important part of the daily routine of the Homes. The bedroom area generally contains space for two to three boys. Note the well-made beds and adjoining desks that provide children with a place for homework and study.

A variety of means was incorporated into the daily structure of the Homes to meet these needs. Initially, the children were placed with loving and caring adults known as "house parents," who would surround them with love and care in an almost grandmotherly fashion. Later, as it was understood that the problems facing the children were far more complex and that changes needed to be made in how those problems were approached, the Home moved from the house parent delivery model to one that encourages the children to define, explore, and develop life goals. The program shifted to the **Teaching-Family Model**, and the adults were called "teaching parents." They continued to fill the traditional role of caregiver in a family setting but also to coordinate and become involved in the child's life and personal goals. The Teaching-Family Model represents an organized method for providing humane, effective, and individualized direction for the children. It is a unique approach that involves meetings with the child and representatives of social service agencies to discuss the needs of the child and to then set about defining goals and strategies for meeting those goals. The approach also includes support systems that will be needed along with any other elements that might enable the child to have a greater opportunity for success. For many of the children, helping them manage behavior is an important goal. A system that provides the children with tangible rewards and consequences is put in place when the child arrives. In the process, the child is totally involved in establishing the rules (because the rules needed are determined by the goals set), changing the rules, reviewing behavior, and understanding how that behavior or response can be improved. Eventually, as the child works to a level of comfort in the Homes, his/her behavior management moves from very close supervision with few privileges to less restrictive supervision and more independent privilege utilization. An important element in the approach to solving the child's problems is the involvement of the family. It is understood that the child is really the symptom of the problem. If real progress is to be made, the family must also be involved, and all family members must learn how to solve the problems that led to the out-of-home placement in the first place. Of course, it is important to note that if it is determined that these problems are unlikely to be solved or if the child has no likelihood of being returned to the home, then Boys and Girls Homes will serve as home for as long as needed. The program serves children aged nine through eighteen (or high school completion).

Foster Care/Adoption

In 1998, the staff of Boys and Girls Homes renewed its commitment to children who might benefit from placement in foster homes and children of different ages than those presently being served in the Cottage or Residential program. Many children and/or sibling groups did not fit into the age ranges served by this program. The Homes was aware of many very young children and even children with children of their own who needed help. For this reason, the Family Foster Care and Adoption Services was begun and at this writing has served more than three hundred children in ten counties across southeastern North Carolina.

The program is administered from offices on the campus of Boys and Girls Homes at Lake Waccamaw and a satellite office located in Kenansville. Staff personnel recruit the foster parents, provide training, place the children, and supervise and support the homes. The program has placed newborn babies, toddlers, elementary-school-aged children, and teenagers. Often, siblings are difficult to place and many times find themselves being split up and placed in different homes or agencies. The Boys and Girls Homes programs make every possible effort to keep siblings together to lessen their problems and facilitate their recovery. In some situations, young teens with children of their own have been taken into the program and placed in foster homes. While a young teen with no means of support may have needs that seem overwhelming, one with a baby has necessarily even greater needs. Boys and Girls Homes Foster Care and Adoption staff have been able to place these children in loving and accepting homes where both can receive support and where the young mother can learn parenting skills that may preclude the possibility of perpetuating the cycle of abuse and neglect often associated with teen mothers. A number of children placed in the foster care homes originally were placed in the residential program but were later found to be better candidates for foster home placement.

Adoptive Care

Placing children in adoptive homes is another program of care now offered by the staff of Boys and Girls Homes. For several years, the Foster Care and Adoption Staff have facilitated the adoption of eligible children. Beginning in 2004, the staff of the Homes was licensed to assume the role of adoption agent. A number of children have been placed thus far. Sometimes, the foster parents adopt the children placed in their homes. At other times, another couple becomes the "forever" or adoptive parents. Children eligible for adoption may be those who are already in the foster care program or those waiting for placement in the program who became eligible when their birth parents terminated their parental rights.

Higher Education

The role of Boys and Girls Homes does not necessarily end with graduation from high school. When children desire to attend college or some post-secondary program, the Homes continues to monitor and to assist the child for as long as is practical and feasible. Moreover, a number of civic club and individual scholarships aid the children in pursuing their dream of a post-secondary education. As of 2005, ninety-one boys and two girls have received bachelor's degrees. Hundreds of others have received associate degrees.

Leadership of Boys & Girls Homes

A. D. Peacock

Founder and First Executive Director (Officially Director) 1954–1958

A. D. Peacock, Founder and Executive Director 1954–1958, with his family. A. D. (left), wife Kathel Lee, son Don and wife Peggy, daughter Linda Lanier and husband Eddie, and the Peacock family grandchildren.

A. D. Peacock was the founder of Boys and Girls Homes of North Carolina. A native of Georgia, Mr. Peacock moved to Columbus County where he was the funeral director of Peacock Funeral Home in Whiteville. Because of the pain he saw in children who had experienced the death of one or both parents and who were left uncared for by that event, he dreamed of establishing a home for such children. He assembled a group of businessmen from the Whiteville community, most of them fellow Civitans, to form a Board of Trustees of "Boys Home" at Lake Waccamaw. Even his most steadfast friends had doubts about this endeavor, but perhaps his greatest attribute was his dedication to establishing the home despite these misgivings. His perseverance paid off, and the Home was founded

At this ceremony recognizing A. D. Peacock as the founder of Boys Home, a plaque was dedicated acknowledging the establishment of the Home. Two of the earliest members of the Boys Home family, Jerry Parrish and Dale Strickland, hold the memorial tablet. The plaque now rests in the roundabout on McCray Lane next to Flemington Hall (the old Gault home).

in 1954. Flemington Hall, the former residence of the F. B. Gault family, provided the initial residence and office of the organization. Mr. Peacock was appointed the first Executive Director and remained in that capacity until the board hired R. N. "Rube" McCray in 1958 to head the operation. *To Save a Boy* is Mr. Peacock's published account of the Home's beginning and its early years. His determination and vision resulted in a home that has served more than three thousand children in residential placements and more than three hundred in foster care and adoptive care. Mr. Peacock died August 4, 1988.

Guiding the Dream

Leadership of Boys & Girls Homes

R. N. "Rube" McCray

Executive Director 1958–1971

R. N. "Rube" McCray, official portrait, Executive Director 1958–1971

Rube McCray, as he was affectionately called, was a native of Tennessee. He had been a successful football coach and athletic director at the College of William and Mary for many years. Prior to coming to Lake Waccamaw in 1956, he had a small car dealership outside Williamsburg, Virginia. However, he felt an urge to work with young people again and thus was receptive when Robert Maultsby, a friend and a member of the Boys Home Board of Trustees, contacted him. The Board thought his experiences working with boys and his fundraising skills would stand him in good stead as the fledgling organization began to grow. Rube and his wife Hester came to Boys Home where he immediately petitioned the major civic organizations in the state to support the boys and provide residences for them. As a result, the Civitans, Lions, Jaycees, Kiwanians, Rotarians, and Optimists built cottages on the campus. It was hard to say no to Rube McCray! He was

Mrs. Hester McCray, Rube, and Mrs. Sanders Dallas, wife of Board Chairman Sanders Dallas. Mrs. McCray was a tremendous supporter of her husband's work at the Home.

a big man—about six feet four inches, with big, multiuse hands that could mete out needed discipline or wrap around a shoulder to offer comfort and love. The boys really admired and respected him, and even today, at alumni meetings, the conversation turns to him. He took a personal interest in each boy and knew everything about him. When McCray was hired, Boys Home actually got two people, as Hester was also very much involved in the campus. She would invite the boys to her house on their birthdays and bake cakes for them. It is told that she even baked pies for the boys to encourage them to make all A's on their report cards! She was also instrumental in getting the North Carolina Federation of Women's Clubs involved in supporting the Home. During his tenure, Mr. McCray was elected president of the National Association of Homes for Children. He directed the campus expansion to include a 108-acre farm at Lake Waccamaw and another campus in Mecklenburg County at Huntersville, prompting the name change to Boys Homes of North Carolina. In November 1971, Mr. McCray died on campus of a heart attack and was buried in his hometown of Greenville, Tennessee. The Lake Waccamaw branch of the Columbus County Library is named in his honor.

Rube in what has become a classic pose. Almost all who remember him note that he had really big hands, hands that could correct or wrap you in comfort as in this photo.

Jerry Parrish was the first Boys Home resident to graduate from high school. In this photo, Rube poses with Jerry commemorating this very special moment in his life and in the life of Boys Home.

Guiding the Dream

Leadership of Boys & Girls Homes

Lester "Les" Craft

Executive Director 1973–1989

Lester R. "Les" Craft, Executive Director 1973–1989. One of the things Mr. Craft understood was the power of the media in promoting the work of the Homes. He often shared stories of the Homes on tele vision and radio and in newspapers.

Following the death of "Rube" McCray in 1971, Mrs. McCray served as acting director until a new director could be employed. Lester R. "Les" Craft, like Rube McCray, was also involved in coaching football, having served as head coach at Georgetown College in Kentucky. In 1973, Les became Executive Director of Boys and Girls Homes. At the time of his appointment, Mr. Craft was married to the former Jean Darter, and they moved to Lake Waccamaw to reside in the upstairs portion of Flemington Hall as Les took over the leadership of the Homes.

Mr. Craft enjoyed sharing Christmas with the children. In this photo, he helps Santa distribute gifts that have been provided for the boys.

Les was very active in the Optimist organization. He joined the Optimist Club of Georgetown, Kentucky, in 1959, serving as its president in 1960–61, and was governor of the Kentucky-West Virginia District of Optimist International. Upon his move to Lake Waccamaw, he joined the Whiteville Optimist Club. On the international level, he served on various committees and was vice president of Optimist International 1976–77, president of Optimist International 1977–78, and executive director of the Optimist International Foundation in St. Louis 1996–98.

Mr. Craft used his organizational skills to expand the operation of Boys and Girls Homes. One significant area of change included the shift from housemothers to house parents. Also during his tenure, the Girls Haven program at Asheboro merged with Boys Home, and the organization became Boys and Girls Homes of North Carolina. The girls program was later moved to the Huntersville campus where it remained for approximately two years. After the Huntersville property was sold, the girls program was consolidated on the campus at Lake Waccamaw.

Jean Craft became ill and died in October of 1985. Later, Les married the former Carolyn Canady, who had been an employee of the Homes. Mr. Craft retired as Executive Director in 1989 and moved to the nearby community of Shallotte in Brunswick County.

Guiding the Dream

Leadership of Boys & Girls Homes

Stuart Sherman

Major General, USAF, Retired, Executive Director/President 1989–2003

Stuart H. Sherman, Major General, USAF, Retired, President/CEO 1989–2003.

Following the retirement of Les Craft in 1989, the Board of Trustees employed Stuart Sherman as the Executive Director of the Homes. Later his title was changed to President/CEO. Before his military retirement, Major General Sherman had worked on numerous satellite programs and construction projects and had commanded Vandenberg Air Force Base. His leadership skills made him an excellent fit for the Homes as it entered a new phase of growth and expansion. During his term, the child-care program adopted the Teaching-Family Model, and every building on the campus underwent either a complete change or modification. Major additions to the physical plant included the Exhibition Center on the farm, the Girls' Activity Center, the Wakefield and Stango Cottages, the Leamon Rogers Memorial Chapel, and the first phase of

In addition to the construction of the Leamon Rogers Memorial Chapel, many of the campus facilities were repaired and refurbished during Stuart Sherman's term as Executive Director/President. In this photo, Sherman (kneeling center) poses on the chapel site with several of the contractors who had a part in its construction.

the Solomon Center. Perhaps the most significant accomplishment of his tenure was the construction and dedication of the Leamon Rogers Memorial Chapel. It was a long-held dream of the Homes to have a place on the campus for a ministry where the children could worship as a family. This perhaps completed the circle of having Boys and Girls Homes provide a family atmosphere for the children who come here.

Mr. Sherman (third from left) and Mrs. Sherman (far right) pose with Al Priest and others at the dedication of the windows in the Leamon Rogers Memorial Chapel. The chapel was a major addition to the Boys and Girls Homes campus, both from a structural and program point of view. Theresa Sherman often assisted her husband in working with the children and in promoting the Homes. One of the activities she engaged in was The Muppet Ministry. Using Muppet characters, the children traveled about telling the story of the Homes at churches and civic club meetings.

Leadership of Boys & Girls Homes

William "Bill" Thompson Jr.

President 2003–present

William H. "Bill" Thompson Jr., President, 2003 to the present

When Stuart Sherman retired, Bill Thompson assumed the duties of president of Boys and Girls Homes where he has held about every position since being hired in 1966. He was the first president/executive director selected who had previously been employed by the organization. Thompson is a native of Hallsboro, a small community adjoining Lake Waccamaw in Columbus County, and a graduate of Campbell College. Most of his career has involved some kind of public relations or fundraising activity as well as a great deal of community involvement. Mr. and Mrs. McCray saw the public relations potential of having a "Boys Choir" that could perform around the state representing Boys Home. Therefore, in the spring of 1966, Mr. McCray contacted Bill Thompson about becoming the music director for Boys Home and organizing a formal choral group to be called "The Boys Home Choir." Thompson

Many former residents remember Bill Thompson for his horsemanship. They fondly tell stories about his prowess with a horse and his encouragement of their own riding and equestrian skills. As an entertainer, Bill Thompson is adept at captivating an audience. Not only an excellent singer, Mr. Thompson is a tremendous writer, composing columns and stories for many local newspapers throughout North Carolina. He writes "Front Porch Stories" for Our State *magazine and has authored two books.*

immediately set about building a program of music involving the children. What he was able to accomplish was phenomenal! Although the choir has not been in existence for years, people still talk about the programs and the boys' talents. Many of the presentations were very elaborate and were performed before special audiences and on television. Bill Thompson has developed numerous public relations strategies and promotional materials for the Homes. Perhaps one of the most noteworthy was a piece entitled "Life Shouldn't Look Like This to a Child," featuring the artwork of one of the Homes boys. He was instrumental in securing property for the farm and establishing a program on that property. He was involved in the construction of the Exhibition Center and establishing an equestrian program on campus. As a writer, he has few equals, publishing pieces weekly in newspapers statewide, writing "Front Porch Stories" for *Our State* magazine, and authoring the books *Sweet Tea, Fried Chicken, and Lazy Dogs* and *Pearl's Pork Palace*. Bill Thompson has taken his position among the legendary leaders of the Homes. As president, he has met a number of challenges, such as a downturn in financial resources following the 9-11 events of 2001 and the tragic death of longtime Vice President for Finance Jeff Spivey on a steely Friday evening in October 2003. Spivey's demise left Thompson without his number one assistant and with a loss of years of information regarding the financial operation of the Homes. To help with Spivey's loss, Thompson coaxed former Director of Planned Giving, Dr. James Jordan, to come out of retirement and assist with the Homes' financial operations. Thompson's resolve to have the Homes continue as a refuge for children and his belief in the people who care about them undergird him as he leads the Homes into its next fifty years of helping children. Thompson's tenure with the Homes gives him an immense knowledge of the Homes' children and supporters. Like Rube McCray, many former residents fondly remember stories about "Bill" or "Mr. Thompson."

Helping the children, both current and former, celebrate their successes is important to Bill. Here he poses with Pat Nolan after Pat's graduation from college—more than fifteen years after high school.

Leadership of Boys & Girls Homes

Board Leadership

Boys Home Executive Committee members, ca. 1962. From left to right: Stacy Budd, E. B. Stone, unknown, James Collier, Dr. W. H. Hoskins, and J. Sanders Dallas.

Boards of Trustees and Directors

Behind each of the great leaders who have taken their place at the helm of Boys and Girls Homes are the Boards of Trustees, or Directors, as they have been known periodically, saying yes, saying no, but generally overseeing and guiding the direction of the Homes from its beginnings to the present. These folks, hundreds in number, have considered the needs of children and worked to support the efforts of the directors and staff and have encouraged others to lend their support to the Homes. Because civic clubs have had such an impact on the work and growth of the Homes, many of the trustees/directors have been representatives of the clubs. As a matter of point, the founding board of Boys Home was made up completely of Civitan members, primarily because A. D. Peacock, a Civitan himself, urged his fellow Civitans' involvement in the beginnings of the Home. Forty-eight people represent their communities, organizations, and the children's best interests on the Board today.

Rube McCray presents information to the Board of Trustees in this 1960s photo. In those days, the meetings were held in what is now the lobby of Flemington Hall. Others in the photo include Chairman J. Sanders Dallas, seated at table center, Mrs. Gold, and James Collier.

Board of Incorporators

These men served as the initial Board of Incorporators for Boys Home. It was their task, working with A. D. Peacock, to do the background work that would lead to the chartering of Boys Home. The Home received its charter December 12, 1954, through their efforts.

James L. Collier
Lee J. Greer
Martin Schulken
W. Crowell Black
Paul Williamson
W. F. Floyd
P. F. Newton
C. Bion Sears
R. G. Maultsby
H. B. Floyd
Dr. Sam Whitehead

The First Officers and Directors

These men, elected by the Board of Incorporators, made up the first Board of Directors of Boys Home. They were responsible for guiding the Home through its early years.

A. D. Peacock, *President*
J. L. "Hap" Collier, *Vice President*
John Ward, *Secretary/Treasurer*
W. Crowell Black, *Director*
W. F. "Bill" Floyd, *Director*
C. Bion Sears, *Director*
Paul Williamson, *Director*
Martin Schulken, *Director*
Lee Greer, *Director*
Dr. Sam Whitehead, *Director*
Bill Hooks, *Director*

Chairmen

The following individuals have presided as Chairman of the Board of Directors/Trustees of Boys and Girls Homes. It was difficult to determine the precise tenure of the earliest chairs. The dates listed are as accurate as possible.

A. D. Peacock *(Acting Chair)*, 1955
James L. "Hap" Collier, 1955-
J. Sanders Dallas Sr., 1959-
E. B. Stone, 1969-
Dorsey Welch, 1976-
Joseph Sandlin, 1978-1981
Carl Bowen, 1981-1984
William A. Horney, 1984-1987
Thomas E. Shreve, 1987-1990
Sanders Dallas Jr., 1990-1992
Charles Waller, 1992-1994
Nancy Phillips, 1994-1996
Lionel Todd, 1996-1998
H. B. Stroup, 1998-2000
Jerry Parrish, 2000-2002
Charles Smith, 2002-2004
Bill Teague, 2004-Present

It was a crowning moment in the history of Boys and Girls Homes when Jerry Parrish, one of the first boys of the Homes, returned to serve as a member of the Board and become its chairman. In this photo, Jerry receives the gavel from outgoing Chairman H. B. Stroup in October 2000.

Boys & Girls Homes Signs

Over the years, Boys and Girls Homes has had a series of signs that denote the organization. Not much is known about the development of them; simply, they depict who and what we are.

Clockwise, from top left: The Boys Home Lake Waccamaw sign on the front lawn in front of Lions Cottage. A photo used in an early Boys Home Christmas card shows Mrs. Maultsby and Rube McCray with several of the boys. The Boys Homes campus sign. Girls Haven campus sign. Former Director of Residential Programs Jimmy Tutor poses with the present-day sign. The Girls Haven sign at the Huntersville facility.

The Children Perform

Ed Miller directs the choir at a performance for the North Carolina General Assembly in this photo made in the Legislative Building in Raleigh.

Sharing the dream of Boys and Girls Homes with others has always been a vital part of fundraising to make the dream a reality for the children. Through the years, there have been the typical visits by members of the staff, letter-writing campaigns, publications, and other assorted efforts to promote the Homes. But without question, the events that more people remember and that generated more sentiment and support were those activities involving the children. Perhaps the most revered of these was the choir. At one time, the Boys Home Choir was almost a household name. Those handsome children with their beautiful voices blended in a harmony that even the angels adored—what mortal could resist? The choir traveled distances far and near to share the reality of Peacock's dream for children, with awesome results. This writer remembers seeing the choir perform and recalls several televised Christmas performances. Obviously, the children worked diligently to produce such delightful musical performances. Clearly, an adult directed and guided those youngsters countless hours to create the beautifully orchestrated shows. So with words borrowed from so many memories, let's take a look back at the choir and its impact on the dream.

Not long after arriving at Boys Home, sometime in the early 1960s, Mrs. Hester McCray, the wife of then-director Rube McCray, invited several of the boys to her residence for an informal sing-along around the piano. Eventually, these informal sessions gave rise to performances for a few of the local civic clubs. In time, Mr. and Mrs. McCray realized the public relations potential of having a "Boys Choir" that could travel and perform representing Boys Home. They needed someone who could give a lot of time to this venture, who possessed knowledge of music, and who had the ability to manage a troupe of energetic boys several hundred miles away from campus. In the spring of 1966, Mr. McCray contacted Bill Thompson about assuming the role of music director for Boys Home and assembling a more formal organization to be called "The Boys Home Choir."

The Boys Home choir, or "Boys Home Singers" as they were affectionately referred to at times, traveled about North Carolina to perform for civic clubs, church groups, and others. Often, though, they performed in Flemington Hall on the Boys Home campus, as in this picture.

Bill Thompson began working immediately with Mrs. McCray and boys living at the Homes to develop a program of music. It was not an easy task. While many of the boys enjoyed music and were eager to participate, their knowledge of music was, at best, minimal. None of the boys could read music; therefore, instruction was by rote. When auditioning the boys, consideration was given to their natural singing ability and the blend of voices. After the boys were selected, they were not allowed to leave the group for any reason, and choir performances took precedence over any other activity.

Most of the boys remained in the choir for the entire duration of their stay at Boys Home, usually two or three years. Practices were held daily including Saturdays during the school year. Mrs. McCray was the accompanist, and on days when Bill Thompson was absent, she conducted the rehearsals.

The choir's programs varied. There was a Christmas program, which was a mixture of sacred and secular music. A spring program emphasized sacred music and was presented in a concert format. Bill Thompson had been a member of the famed Campbell College Touring Choir, and Mrs. McCray undoubtedly had attended numerous choir performances at the College of William and Mary. Perhaps this explains why the model for the Boys Home Choir was a college chorus. The choir performed primarily for civic clubs but also traveled around North Carolina during the Christmas season and performed "live" on television stations across the state.

When the boys performed, they were not a ragtag bunch! Great efforts were made to ensure that the choir members looked every bit as good as they sounded. The standard choir uniform was a blue blazer, grey slacks, a white shirt, and a red tie. Each boy was responsible for maintaining his own uniform. On occasion, they also performed in a variety of less formal outfits suitable for a particular show's theme. For example, if their performance had a country flavor, the boys might wear country attire including cowboy hats and bandannas.

The boys had a tremendous opportunity to perform as they demonstrated their talents on the steps of the U.S. Capitol and at the Jefferson Memorial in 1981.

The choir offered a variety of entertainers from among its numbers. There were soloists and a small ensemble group of six boys that performed to the accompaniment of two guitars. They sang popular and folk music.

The stories of the choir evoke many memories and nearly always include getting to and from the performances. Transportation to performances was usually in three station wagons owned by the Home and driven by Bill Thompson, Rube McCray, and one of the boys. An activity bus was also used to travel to the performances. Those trips call forth colorful remembrances, some truer than others, but we'll leave those to the memories of the choir members!

In 1969, it was decided that there needed to be a person who could devote his time solely to the music program, and Ed Miller was appointed as the first full-time music director for the Homes. Mr. Miller and his wife Katie were both passionate musicians. Both had degrees from Westminster Choir College, and Mrs. Miller had a degree from Penn State University. Mr. Miller attended a Fred Waring Music Workshop shortly after coming to Boys Home, which helped mold his work with the Boys Home Choir. In addition to the choir, Ed was also responsible for the school music program, and he and Katie arranged to give extra time to those boys who needed help learning music for concerts. Mrs. Miller was also the accompanist for the choir, and she worked with some of the boys interested in learning to play the piano.

Under the Millers' direction, the general program and schedule of training remained the same but with an emphasis on development of individual talents. The Millers developed a more relaxed performing style and placed less emphasis on the sacred music. They organized the first junior choir, which was an outgrowth of the school music program. Now, the older, more mature voices were in one group, and the younger voices comprised the junior choir. At one time, there were as many as thirty boys participating in each choir. In addition, the choir performances expanded to include more instrumental music. Katie Miller formed the Boys Homes Bell Choir, and performances were rearranged to include them, primarily during the Christmas season. The Millers also added robes to the choir uniform.

By June of 1971, the Millers had left the program, and Leslie Sullivan was hired as music director. His duties were the same as Ed Miller's, including the school music program. Leslie was a graduate of Campbell College with a degree in organ and music education. He produced the same kinds of programs involving the senior and junior choirs and the bell choir. As many as seventy boys (more than half the campus population) were involved in some kind of musical performing group. During that time, the average size of the two choirs was about fifty boys, and the average length of stay by a boy was two and a half years.

Leslie had one full-time accompanist, Bill Ruth, who was also the local Methodist minister. Bill attended all rehearsals and traveled with the senior choir, all at his own expense. Gene Burns, who was the civic club coordinator at that time, accompanied the junior choir and the senior choir when Bill Ruth was unable to go. The number of performances increased during this period to nearly one hundred a year! When the schedule became so hectic that the groups were slated for performances in different locations on the same day, the station wagons were abandoned in favor of the activity bus. The formal uniform of the choir remained the traditional blue blazers.

By 1975, Leslie Sullivan left the program, and Rodney and Sandra Douglas were hired to lead the music program. Both graduates of Campbell College with degrees in church music, they were responsible for the same duties as the previous directors. They resigned after only six months, and Gene Burns was appointed choir director while Bill Ruth continued as accompanist. Gene also remained civic club coordinator.

In June of 1976, Linza Smith was hired as music director, assistant choir director, and accompanist. Linza was a graduate of Meredith College with a degree in music education and was the first female to serve as music director. Linza and Gene continued the choir program in the same style as in the past, with one exception. The Christmas television show was taped at WSOC-TV in Charlotte and sent to other stations throughout the state, thus eliminating the travel to each individual station.

In the spring of 1979, Sharyn McSwain served as accompanist for a brief time. Gene Burns resigned in the fall of 1979, and Ed and Katie Miller returned briefly to work with the choir through the Christmas season. A volunteer from Trinity Baptist Church in Whiteville served as choir director during the early months of 1980.

This choir group was established to participate in a fiftieth anniversary celebration held in Pinehurst in May 2004.

Upon his employment in September 1980, Jimmie Tutor, a Campbell College and Southeastern Theological Seminary graduate, assumed the full-time duties of choir director and the responsibility of the school music program. Tutor reorganized the music program to only one choir, usually made up of sixteen to eighteen boys. Jimmie was

Mrs. Green and Mrs. Sherman stand in front of the collection of Muppets that were used by the Boys and Girls Homes Muppeteers as they shared the story of the Homes.

his own accompanist and also directed the bell choir. For occasions when the full choir wasn't available, Tutor had developed a quartet that could perform admirably. Under Tutor's guardianship, the spring program became a patriotic presentation, and the Christmas television show was staged on location at Boys Home for the first time in 1985. The last bell choir performance was in 1987. The apparel for the choir changed to brown corduroy suits for the winter and blue blazers with tan slacks for spring. Although the choir continued to travel by bus, vans were part of the campus fleet and were used on occasion. Tutor continued to work with the choir as he divided his time as a social worker with the Home. In the early 1990s, the number of choir engagements and associated travel diminished increasingly although there is evidence of at least one program presented in February of 1991 when the choir performed patriotic music. By the end of that year, the formal Boys (and Girls) Home Choir was dissolved, and Boys and Girls Homes School assumed the regular school music program. Various efforts have been made in the years since to revive the choir of the "glory" years but with little success. The children's average length of stay at the Homes has decreased, making it harder to attract them to the program and more difficult to train their voices and them as choir members. The era of the Boys Home Choir was a significant part of the history of the Homes and in itself could be the subject of an entire book! No doubt the performers and the audiences have great memories of this tremendous part of the Homes experience.

Theresa Sherman, wife of Executive Director Stuart Sherman, and Mary Ann Green, wife of Bill Green, campus director, were responsible for developing another Boys and Girls Homes story-sharing effort. During the early years of the Girls Haven program in Asheboro, the girls became involved in a therapy program using puppets. As an extension of that effort, Mrs. Sherman and Mrs. Green developed a Muppet program in which the children performed and told stories of the Homes with Muppets. The children traveled to civic club and other meetings for their performances. The program was quite a production during the mid-nineties, performing for a number of audiences. Again, as the length of stay by the children decreased, the Muppet program began to phase out. The last televised performance for a choir and Muppet troupe occurred during Christmas 2003 when a program of music, Muppets, and recitation was taped on location at Boys and Girls Homes and distributed to television stations across North and South Carolina.

Other Notable Staff & Board Members

Here, Mrs. Doris Wagner, manager of the Boys and Girls Homes Country Store, holds one of the numerous pieces of artwork donated to the Homes by Art.com of Cary, North Carolina. The company decided to discontinue its framed art business and to donate its inventory. As happens in many cases for Boys and Girls Homes, an Art.com employee whose grandmother had ties to Boys and Girls Homes suggested that the company consider the Homes. As a result, Art.com donated several thousand pieces of framed and unframed prints that were sold through the Country Store with the proceeds benefiting the residents of the Homes.

In the course of fifty years, many people have walked on the campus of Boys and Girls Homes. Their footprints have marked the path that has led many children to more productive lives. It would be impossible to list them all, but it would be a mistake not to try. The names of those who left deeper footprints follow.

Staff

Willie Adcock—Head of maintenance for many years during the 1960s.

Chip Barnes—Began working as farm manager in the 1970s.

Lois Blackwell—Employed in the early 1970s to work in financial resources. Later moved to childcare where she continues to serve.

Laura Bordeaux—Longtime employee in the finance/accounting program.

Bonnie Wise Brown—Employed in the 1960s to work in the donor program. Bonnie was killed in a tragic auto accident.

Sherry Brown—Employed in the early 1970s to work in the donor program. Continues to work as switchboard operator.

Jack Burgess—A native of Tennessee and graduate of North Carolina State. He was campus director at Lake Waccamaw and later was the first director at Huntersville.

Fanny Burleson—Longtime principal of Boys Homes School.

Gene Burns—Schoolteacher, civic club coordinator, and music director during the 1970s.

Carolyn Canady Craft—Secretary to Mr. McCray and Mr. Craft.

Carol Ramey Carlson—Wrote most of the promotional material during the 1970s and 1980s.

Rob Conway—Campus coordinator and vocational instructor during the 1970s and early 1980s.

Carl Dean—Unit director in the 1980s.

Shirley Dean—Worked with husband Carl as house parents in Kiwanis Cottage in the 1980s.

Agnes Delaney—Head bookkeeper for many years.

Carolyn Dudley—Wife of Leon Dudley and a cook on the campus, mostly in the Civitan Cottage, for many years. Mrs. Dudley died in December 2005.

Leon Dudley—Has been continuously employed by Boys and Girls Homes in the maintenance and groundskeeping department since the early 1960s.

Gary Faircloth—Former resident who returned as a social worker on the Huntersville campus and later became Director of Development.

Ron Faircloth—Gary's brother. First Boys Home resident to graduate from college. Worked on the staff during the 1970s.

Numerous adults have been part of the program of care provided by Boys and Girls Homes. Some have only a brief tenure with the Homes, and their impact is fleeting at best. Others, like Leon Dudley pictured here trimming the acres of grass that are a part of the Boys and Girls Homes campus, have a more profound impact on and relationship with the children who come to the Homes. Leon has been a member of the Homes' staff since the early sixties and has watched a number of the young people grow up. As former residents return to the Homes for a visit or to attend an alumni gathering, one of the first persons they ask about is Leon. Leon's wife Carolyn was also employed by the Homes as a cook, and she too had an impact on many of the residents, who declare adamantly that she was the best cook to ever grace a kitchen at Boys Home. They especially remember the fried chicken dinners she made and the special treats she provided that made their stay seem more like home!

Danny Gore—Unit director in the 1980s.

Louise Gore—Housemother in the Rotary Cottage.

Shirley Hairston—Longtime employee of the maintenance/housekeeping staff.

Randy Harrell—First assistant director.

Bill Hughes—First athletic director.

Dr. James Jordan—Worked at Boys and Girls Homes during two different periods. During his first tenure, he worked in Financial Development in the area of Planned Giving. He returned to Boys and Girls Homes in 2004 to become executive vice president.

Marie Kelly—Employed in the early 1970s. She continues to work in institutional advancement.

Mary Maultsby—Housemother in the Lions Cottage.

Doug McConnell—Unit director in the 1980s.

Hester McCray—Wife of Rube McCray. She was in charge of much of the promotional activities in the early years and organized the first singing group on the campus. She would always bake a cake for each boy's birthday.

Regena Edwards McNair—Bookkeeper and personnel officer for many years.

George McRae—Athletic director during the early 1970s.

Ed and Katie Miller—Ed was the music director, and Katie was his assistant during the 1970s.

Bill Morrison—Longtime staff member. Began as a social worker in late 1960s. Still works with the higher education program.

Kyle Ramey—Campus director during the 1970s and early 1980s.

Henry Sadler—Campus director during the early 1970s.

Shirley Sasser—Secretary to Mr. McCray, Mr. Craft, Mr. Sherman, and Mr. Thompson.

Doris Sealey—Headed the donor management program for many years.

Loren Soft—Residential director for the Huntersville campus. In charge of financial development during the 1970s and early 1980s.

Jeff Spivey—Pictured at left, served Boys and Girls Homes for twenty years, many as vice president for finance. Jeff was killed in a head-on automobile collision en route home from work October 3, 2003.

Addie Lee Stanley—Employed in the 1960s to work in the donor program.

J. L. Stanley—Worked in campus maintenance and was later first farm manager.

Eleanor Turner—Longtime employee in the donor program.

Roy Walker—Civic club coordinator during the 1980s and 1990s.

"Mom" and "Pop" Wingfield—House parents on the Lake Waccamaw and Huntersville campuses.

Board of Trustees

Crowell Black—One of the founding members of the board and a major contributor.

Nick Boddie—Member of the Executive Committee and a major contributor.

Dr. Carl Bowen—Past chairman and a major promoter of Boys and Girls Homes in the Optimist Club.

Stacy Budd—A Lion. Was Chairman of the Board and provided tires for all the vehicles on campus.

Judge Coleman Cates—Juvenile court judge from Burlington and a Lion. Served as vice chairman of the Board. Coleman Cates Award named in his honor.

J. L. "Hap" Collier—Treasurer and Chairman of the Board.

Sanders Dallas Sr.—Early Chairman of the Board and major donor.

Bill Horney—Chairman of the Board and one of the largest contributors.

Elbert Mallard—Longtime member of the board and a Civitan.

Joe Sandlin—Chairman of the Board and a longtime financial advisor to the board.

Edgar Stevens—A Lion. A major donor who loved to visit the children.

E. B. Stone—From Charlotte. Served five continuous terms as Chairman of the Board.

Dan Todd—Chairman of the Executive Board and very active local supporter.

Dorsey Welch—A Rotarian. Served as Chairman of the Board during the early expansion of the lake campus.

A Former Resident Remembers

Former residents of Boys Home, Jerry Parrish, Jimmy Boone, and Tom Simmons, talk at an annual alumni gathering held on the campus of Boys and Girls Homes on the second weekend of October. Jerry Parrish was a Boys Home resident from 1958 to 1961 and now resides in Henderson, North Carolina. He holds the distinction of being the first resident of Boys Home to graduate from high school. Jerry served as a member of the Boys and Girls Homes Board of Directors and was board chairman from 2000 to 2002. Jimmy Boone lived at Boys Home from 1961 to 1964 and now dwells in Ashland, Virginia. Tom Simmons, a Boys Home resident from 1958 to 1964, now lives in Boiling Spring Lakes, North Carolina. Tom is a retired educator and spent the last years of his career as a high school principal—quite a turnaround for a young man brought to Boys Home because he wouldn't go to school! He too has served as a member of the Boys and Girls Homes Board of Trustees, chairing the alumni committee. The gatherings of the alumni are tremendous events and are particularly interesting for non-alumni as alums recount their adventures while living at the Home. Sometimes it is difficult to distinguish fact from fiction!

In this note, former Boys Home resident David Herring remembers his time at the Homes in an email to his Boys Home brothers.

This is an Old Geezer's Recollection from 40 years ago:

Kitchen Duty. The cottages each had 16 boys and 1 housemother. Each week, the boys would rotate the duties so that 4 at a time would do each set of duties. The 4 assigned KP or Kitchen Duty would (I think) be responsible for each meal, which included 7 breakfasts, 2 weekend lunches, and 7 dinners. I believe 1 boy would do the dishes, 1 would do pots & pans, 1 would clear table and sweep/mop kitchen floor, and 1 would get up 30 minutes earlier than the rest and help prepare breakfast. I think all would get up at 6:30, so I guess the early guy was at 6 a.m.

The boy helping prepare breakfast would spread bread on 2 or more cookie sheets and cook butter in a pan. He would then spread the melted butter over the bread with a special brush. Then stick cookie sheets in oven.

Wake up. I am thinking 6:30. Housemother would walk down the hall, ringing that bell. Or sometimes beating on a pan. I believe we ate at 7 a.m. Did cottage chores at 7:30 and the bus at 8, I believe.

Morning jobs. 2 guys carried slop to the hogs. Can't remember how they fit in on the rotation, though. A boy swept & mopped the living room. Another boy did the same with the dining room, and another did the same with the "hobby room." Another did the same with the hallway and "mud room." I am thinking there was also a room, but also think that may have been a central place on campus, somewhere. One of the boys in each room took a week sweeping & mopping the bedroom. Another did the bathroom.

As you can see, I don't remember exactly how those jobs got divided among the 16 boys.

A Columbus County school bus stayed on campus, and one of the boys would drive. When there were more boys there, we had a second school bus, I believe. The ride would be very slow, and we would often yell at the girls waiting for their bus.

Does anyone remember the safety ritual practiced by the bus driver? During my time there, there was actually a train track next to the highway that would have several trains per day running. The driver was required to stop short of the track; a boy would jump off the bus and run across the track, then wave the bus across. He would then get back on.

The school was old THEN, and is still operating now. I remember sitting in class, watching the plaster fall from the ceiling, onto the teacher's desk. Popular classes at that time [were] Home Ec for the girls and vocational agriculture for the boys. A popular contest each year was the "greased pig"-tackling event. It also involved mud.

I took "typing" class. We would be given [a] class assignment, which I never did. I would always write stories, making fun of the Boys Home staff, complete with nicknames—along with boys who would be heroes, playing pranks on the men, etc. The boys would always look forward to my day's story, and someone would read it aloud on the bus ride home. I was always careful to keep up with it and destroy it before we got back on campus.

Work and Exercise. Mr. McCray, Mr. Harrell, Mr. Burgess, Mr. Adcock, and Mr. Dew would meet the bus next to the Big House and give us our work assignments for the afternoon. Some of us would somehow get a disproportionate share of unpleasant work assignments. (I believe someone is still whining, here.) I often found myself cleaning land in the swamp or working in the garden with Mr. Adcock. Some of the boys got the easy work...in the cottages. After a quick snack and dropping one's books in their rooms, we worked from about 3:30 p.m. until 5 p.m. At 5, we went to the athletic field for 1 hour exercise.

The cottages were very clean. As well as the fields and lawns on campus. The Hallsboro sports teams were monopolized by Boys Home boys who were in better physical shape than the other kids, due to our exercise and work routines. Hallsboro teams usually whipped up on the other schools that had considerably more students.

Free Time. We ate dinner at 6, and had free time until Study Hall at 7. Free time was for the boys who did not have kitchen duties after dinner. We sat at our desks and foot of our beds for study hall, unless we chose to sit at [the] dining room table or [on] a living room chair. [Messrs.] McCray, Harrell, Dew, Adcock, etc. would wander through the cottages, making sure we were making good use of our study time. I believe study hall went until 9:30. Then there was 30 minutes free time before lights out at 10.

Mr. McCray would often make rounds well after lights out. No one would hear him coming; he would just randomly pick a room and turn on the light, often catching boys either not in their beds, or up to something.

Anyway, I am a little fuzzy on some details, but I'll bet you are too, so...that is my story, and I'm sticking to it.

-David H-

A Celebration of Fifty Years of Service to Children

On December 12, 2004, during Boys and Girls Homes' annual Christmas Open House observance, the program included a celebration of fifty years of service to children. In ceremonies held in the Leamon Rogers Memorial Chapel, Boys and Girls Homes observed its fifty years as a home for children by recognizing past directors, members of the first Board of Directors, the first teaching parents, board chairmen, and the role of civic clubs in the history of the Homes. President Bill Thompson presented a commemorative plaque to Dr. Sam Whitehead, a member of the original Board of Directors of Boys Homes. The agenda for the ceremony follows along with a letter of invitation to special invitees.

Boys and Girls Homes of North Carolina
50th Anniversary Celebration

History

Recognition of Past Directors

A. D. Peacock
R. N. "Rube" McCray
Lester "Les" Craft
Stuart Sherman
Bill Thompson

Recognition of First Board Members (as listed in Mr. Peacock's book)

Board of Incorporators
James L. Collier
Lee J. Greer
Martin Schulken
W. Crowell Black
Paul Williamson
W. F. Floyd
P. F. Newton
C. Bion Sears
R. G. Maultsby
H. B. Floyd
Dr. Sam Whitehead

Officers and Directors (elected by Board of Incorporators)
A. D. Peacock, President
J. L. "Hap" Collier, Vice President
John Ward, Secretary/Treasurer
W. Crowell Black, Director
W. F. "Bill" Floyd, Director
C. Bion Sears, Director
Paul Williamson, Director
Martin Schulken, Director
Lee Greer, Director
Dr. Sam Whitehead, Director
Bill Hooks, Director

Recognition of First Teaching Parents

Mr. and Mrs. A. B. Dawsey Sr.

Recognition of Board Chairmen

A. D. Peacock (Acting Chair), 1955
James L. "Hap" Collier, 1955-
J. Sanders Dallas Sr., 1959-
E. B. Stone, 1969-
Dorsey Welch, 1976-
Joseph Sandlin, 1978-1981
Carl Bowen, 1981-1984
William A. Horney, 1984-1987
Thomas E. Shreve, 1987-1990
Sanders Dallas Jr., 1990-1992
Charles Waller, 1992-1994
Nancy Phillips, 1994-1996
Lionel Todd, 1996-1998
H. B. Stroup, 1998-2000
Jerry Parrish, 2000-2002
Charles Smith, 2002-2004

Recognition of Civic Clubs

Civitan—built cottage 1958 (Jr. Civitans)
Lions—built cottage 1960 (Leos)
Jaycees—built cottage 1962 (?)
Kiwanis—built cottage 1964 (Builder's Club, Key Club, Circle K)
Rotary—built cottage 1966 (Interact)
Optimist—built cottage 1968 (Jr. Optimists)

Extension & Community Association
General Federation of Women's Clubs of North Carolina (Jr. Women)
Ruritan

Closing Remarks

This letter is one of several sent to special guests (in this case the family of A. D. Peacock) in observance of the fiftieth anniversary of Boys and Girls Homes.

December 1, 2004

Peggy, Donnie, Kyle and Craig Peacock
Peacock's Chapel In The Pines Funeral Home
Hwy 701 Business
Whiteville, NC 28472

Dear Peggy, Donnie, Kyle, and Craig:

December 2004 represents a significant milestone in the history of Boys and Girls Homes of North Carolina. It is the Homes' 50th anniversary! During our first fifty years, more than 3,500 children have been helped by having a warm and loving place to live, the guidance of concerned and caring staff members, shelter from the storms of life, good food and clothing, educational and vocational experiences, and opportunities for spiritual growth.

At our annual Christmas Open House on December 12, 2004, we will celebrate our fifty years of service to children! In ceremonies in the Leamon Rogers Memorial Chapel, we plan to recognize some who have played a significant role in that service to the children.

Please join me in the Leamon Rogers Memorial Chapel at three o'clock p.m. on Sunday, December 12, as we pay tribute to fifty great years of caring for the children of Boys and Girls Homes of North Carolina.

Sincerely,

Bill Thompson, Jr.
President/CEO

Continuing the Dream

The Future

The board and staff of Boys Home (and now Boys and Girls Homes) early on knew the importance of an education for the children's future. From that belief, they encouraged the children to study and to do well in school. Study hall and tutoring sessions were always a part of the Homes' regimen to help the children complete and understand their homework and other school assignments. Since the early years of the Home, both an annual awards program to celebrate achievements and recognition services for high school and college graduates have been held. In this photo, Boys Home Director Rube McCray proudly recognizes the graduation of Jerry Parrish from Hallsboro High School; Jerry was the first Boys Home resident to graduate from high school.

The story of Boys and Girls Homes is more than a few recollections of how a number of needy children were brought to a place, given a bed to sleep in and clothing to wear, compelled to attend school and church, assigned chores, and urged to go to ball practice, choir practice, and any number of other "practices." It is more than the efforts of one man to create a place where those things could occur. It is more than the support given by countless groups and individuals to help build and then grow the place. But it is those things, too! In the fifty plus years of Boys and Girls Homes, more than 3,500 children have come through its doors, and each has a story. Those who have helped the children with their stories, either as staff members or as contributors to the programs of care, have memories of a smile, an achievement, a reunion, or a new life. All of these are part of the greater story that is Boys and Girls Homes. Perhaps there will come a time when there is no longer a need for a Boys and Girls Homes. Until that story is written, however, Boys and Girls Homes must continue to exist, to develop its programs around the needs of the children, and to make "a difference to that one" and to all who seek comfort and shelter among the pecan trees on the shores of Lake Waccamaw. Boys and Girls Homes commends all the young people who have been a part of the story for their efforts to "create a new story" and become contributing citizens of the greater story. The Homes thanks all past and current staff members, board members, and contributors who have made a home for the children possible.